DESIGN SCHOOL WISDOM

DESIGN SCHOOL WISDOM

Make First, Stay Awake, and Other Essential Lessons for Work and Life

EDITED BY
Brooke Johnson and Jennifer Tolo Pierce

CHRONICLE BOOKS
SAN FRANCISCO

To all of our teachers, with admiration and respect.
And to our parents—our first and greatest teachers.

Library of Congress Cataloging-in-Publication Data available.

ISBN: 978-1-4521-1531-3

Manufactured in China.

Design by Brooke Johnson and Jennifer Tolo Pierce

10 9 8 7 6 5 4 3 2 1

Chronicle Books LLC
680 Second Street
San Francisco, CA 94107

www.chroniclebooks.com

ACKNOWLEDGMENTS

Our deepest gratitude goes to everyone who helped to make this book a reality. First and foremost, the contributors: Debbie Adams; Bob Aufuldish; Kermit Bailey; Jessica Barness; Brad Bartlett; Leslie Becker; Rachel Berger; Marta Bernstein; Marco Campedelli; May Chung; John V. Clarke; Peter Cocking; Dennis Crowe; Lou Danziger; Natalie Davis; Melanie Doherty; Jason Dubin; Elliott Earls; Patrick FitzGerald; Mark Fox; Leslie Friesen; John Gambell; Roderick Grant; Cheri Gray; Tina Hardison; Eric Heiman; Amber Howard; Dan Hoy; Mariko Jesse; Walter Jungkind; Brett MacFadden; Emily McVarish; KT Meaney; Leigh Mignogna; N. Silas Munro; Charles Nix; Lindsay Nohl; Jayme Odgers; Kevin Paolozzi; Clive Piercy; Andy Pressman; Hank Richardson; Martha Scotford; Doug Scott; Liz Selbert; Ben Shaykin; Steven Skaggs; Andrew Sloat; Carol Sogard; Michael Vanderbyl; Petrula Vrontikis; Pirco Wolfframm; Angie Wang; Franz Werner; and Maranatha Wilson. Thank you for generously sharing not only your words of wisdom but also your passion for and commitment to design education.

Many thanks, as well, to those who introduced us to or otherwise helped connect us with design teachers throughout North America and beyond: Sandro Berra; Marta Castrosin; Michael Carabetta; Emily Dubin; Neil Egan; Laura Howell; Eloise Leigh; Lauren Smith; and Allison Weiner. It's not always about who you know, but sometimes knowing a certain someone can really help.

Last but not least, this book would not have been possible without the support and dedication of the Chronicle Books team: Lia Brown, Yolanda Cazares, Caitlin Kirkpatrick, Diane Levinson, Peter Perez, Leigh Saffold, Erin Thacker, and Bridget Watson Payne. Thank you for believing in this project from concept to final book and for your encouragement and guidance along the way.

"Think it's all been done before? No one has done this in your unique voice, at this time, in this context. Be authentic and do it anyway."

—JESSICA BARNESS
School of Visual Communication Design
Kent State University

INTRODUCTION

"Design school." For many designers, those two words immediately conjure the experience of plunging into new territory, of grasping (not even close to mastering) the strangely unfamiliar vernacular of design, of standing with jaws on the floor before flashes of true design genius, of late nights and passionate experimentation, of epic failures and surprising successes. Design school may mean undergraduate study or graduate, low residency or full time on location. It may mean a class or two to refine an instinctive talent, or it may even mean on-the-job learning (sometimes the best kind of learning there is). Whatever the outside package, the overall experience is ultimately the same (with variations)—the experience of evolving from a nondesigner into a designer. Throughout this experience, there are the words of the design teachers and mentors that lift up, tell it straight, and otherwise guide young designers into their own. These words are the pearls of design school wisdom, words that need only be uttered once to be remembered for a lifetime.

Design School Wisdom was born out of a desire to share the wisdom of design instructors with designers everywhere—students just entering their studies or recent design school graduates starting their first jobs, designers well into their careers or seasoned pros who still can benefit from the wisdom of their peers. We asked teachers and students from across the country and beyond for their pearls of design school wisdom, and we received varied and enthusiastic replies. As this book has taken shape, we have been continually inspired both by the words themselves and by the spirit in which they are shared.

Design teachers and mentors are a dedicated group, and whether their words in the classroom are intentionally imparted or blasted in a fit of design passion and enthusiasm, their students listen, their fresh minds soaking up every word. Ask any designer to quote you something a teacher said in design school, and she will have at least one example that has lodged in her design brain forever.

In addition to inspirational adages, *Design School Wisdom* also shares in-depth perspectives on design education and educators. Some essays address multiple topics—from defining "design education" to inspiring accounts of teachers who have played major roles in a particular designer's development (and influenced her own path as a teacher). There are interviews between students and their instructors that reveal both different approaches to teaching and the unique relationships that form between student and teacher within the world of design education and practice. There is no right or wrong way to approach this book. Read it cover to cover, or dive in at random. Experience it as you would walking through a traditional design school— attend a popular lecture, join an animated discussion, eavesdrop on the teachers' words punctuating the intense focus of the design school environment. Have fun. Listen in. Share what you hear. Add your own words of wisdom to the mix. Above all, be inspired.

Design education doesn't ever end, even after many, many years of professional practice. The best part of that education, though, happens when your mind is open and eager to learn, when everything is new, and when you see only the potential of great things to come.

"ALWAYS BE LEARNING."

—CHARLES NIX

Parsons The New School for Design

"THE SOLUTION TO EVERY PROBLEM LIES WITHIN THE PROBLEM ITSELF."

—JAYME ODGERS
California Institute of the Arts

"Most of the work you do will be for the average person. Don't separate yourself from society so much that you forget what it's like to live life."

—JASON DUBIN
Art Center College of Design

"Don't make it look like you got Photoshop for Christmas."

—KERMIT BAILEY
North Carolina State University
College of Design

"CONTRAST IS YOUR FRIEND."

—BOB AUFULDISH
California College of the Arts

Admiration: John Gambell :: *by Rachel Berger*

My subject today is admiration. Whom or what do I admire, and how has that influenced my work and process?

I think admiration is one of the all-time great feelings. Less toxic than envy, less somber than respect, less extreme than worship, admiration is reserved, yet wonderful. It is sweet without being saccharine. It is thoughtful without being intellectual. It's a deceptively sophisticated feeling—almost Victorian, with its buttoned-up surface disguising a deep well of feeling. It feels like a term favored by Jane Austen or George Eliot to describe a quivering young love affair.

What or whom do I admire? That's easy. I admire all sorts of things. Tartine's morning buns. Ke$ha's style. Michelle Obama's arms. *Friday Night Lights.* The San Francisco Giants and their terrible hair. Eames rocking chairs. Backup dancers, brain surgeons, and pioneers. But most of all, I admire this man: John Gambell.

John Gambell is the university printer at Yale, which is sort of like being the university's design director. He also teaches typography every fall in Yale's MFA graphic design program. His was the most important class I took in graduate school.

THE DAGGER

First Impressions

My first impression of John was that he was a complete square, thoroughly conservative, and likely to disapprove of most things.

With his tweed ties and blazers, blue oxford shirts, and pressed pants, he perfectly embodied my idea of a Yale man, and he looked nothing like someone I'd come to art school to learn from. The first couple weeks of class, my classmates and I would pin up various exercises, and John would make small, horrified gasping sounds, collect himself, and then start the crit. We cringed and cursed ourselves and our stupidity. We cursed him, too, for being so calm, and speaking so carefully, and having such a firm idea of what was right and what was not right, and for withholding that from us.

Soon we realized that John was not to be so easily written off. Because of how straitlaced, almost prim, he seemed, we were eager to discover his dark side. Rumors abounded about John's life outside of school. We heard he had a penchant for motorcycles and leather jackets, stand-up canoeing and Israeli martial arts. That he had worked as a fish processor before becoming a graphic designer, that he was building a miniature house in Vermont, that he was an accomplished painter. We learned that some former students called him "the gambler" and his son "the gambino." Our mild-mannered professor was starting to seem like Clark Kent, a superhero wrapped in herringbone.

Child Labor

As we got to know John, it was clear that despite his wild side, we weren't wrong to think him fastidious, judgmental, and rigorous. Two mornings a week, we watched him calmly break off hunks of breakfast breads and drink coffee while telling us how type and letters worked. We learned that he prefers Univers to Helvetica, open leading to tight, the appropriate and exact use of terms like "modern" and "contemporary." John was big on the penultimate draft. We would make twenty versions of a book, bring it into the review thinking we were finally done, and John would say, "No, no, this is just the penultimate draft." We heard that he taught his children to perfect bind their book reports, that when he was a student in a workshop with Bradbury Thompson and they had to cut up old ship engravings to use to make compositions, John *couldn't do it* because he thought the engravings were too beautiful. We took his recommendations to buy a pica ruler and a copy of Bringhurst's

Elements of Typographic Style, to use Stempel Garamond or ITC Century for children's books, and to dust the fore-edges of accordion-folded books with talcum powder.

Hunter-Gatherers

We became accustomed to John's face turning pale when he looked at a page of relatively inoffensive student type, and when he began, in slow, measured, even pained words to try to make us see that there was just too much space between the words. It was as if he were just too sensitive to handle looking at poor H&Js (which stands for "Hyphenation and Justification" in reference to typesetting words within a paragraph). Like a prospector biting gold, John would take hold of a chapbook someone had been working on for weeks, rub the cover between his thumb and index finger, and shudder if he found the stock to be "too boardy." John's physical horror at poor typography was legendary. Thumbing through another small book, he turned a page and jumped back, revolted. Quickly composing himself, John looked up and said, "Please set quotations and apostrophes with typographer's quotes. . . . When you don't . . . it's like a . . ." (he moved his glasses, obviously nauseated) "a dagger in my eye."

John told us wild stories: "Imagine you are a hunter-gatherer. You trudge through the woods, spy a boar, and give chase. You hurl a spear, bring it down, and finish it off with a hatchet. You hoist it upon your back and trudge home. You then lay the beast down before your hunter-gatherer family and they are awed. This is analogous to a spread with some particularly nice visual, which the reader experiences after having trudged through pages of dry text and minimal imagery."

We used his name as a verb—to "John Gambell" a piece of design was to manually shorten em dashes, space small caps, use the proper ligatures, eliminate double spaces, fix and refix rags. These were all small details, but we internalized the lesson that they were practically sacred—that such details matter fundamentally in good design. My second year in studio, someone made a poster that had a simple line drawing of John with his glasses slid slightly off his nose, analyzing a piece of design. Underneath sat the text "WWJGD" in large, bold letters.

"You might think you're an artist, but you're not."

Along with Doug Scott and Chris Pullman, John is one of the three wise men of Yale's program. They have all taught there for more than twenty-five years. They are all graduates of the Yale of Paul Rand, Armin Hofmann, Alvin Lustig, and the great modernists. Even as a graduate student, John's nature was evident. Paul Rand once said to him, "Gambell, you're a very conservative designer." John said, "Yeah. I think for the most part design is a lot of noise about nothing. I prefer to be a bit straightforward." Rand said, "Yeah you're right. Too bad more people don't think that way." John is the only of the three wise men who lives in New Haven, not far from campus, and who works for the university full time.

As university printer, John's two best-known accomplishments have been partnering with Matthew Carter to develop the Yale typeface and implementing a comprehensive signage program for the university. The typeface has John written all over it: Gambell-sanctioned em dashes and thoughtful features like small caps for web use and the word "Yale" as its own character, perfectly kerned.

The signs showcase the typeface beautifully, but they are also reflective of John's great non-snobbery. For years, Yale followed a policy of "If you can't find your way here, you don't belong here," but the signage program made the university accessible to anyone. John's most important campaign may be his effort to cultivate an appreciation of good design throughout the university. He offers free consultation services to Yale departments to help them reduce costs while increasing graphic and editorial effectiveness. He also leads tutorials about Yale's graphic identity, typography, editing, and design and publications management for any group of Yale employees who are interested.

John was not someone who knew he wanted to be a graphic designer from childhood, but it isn't hard to see how he got there. As a dreamy kid, John drew outlandish contraptions such as crazy diagrams demonstrating how to make a rocket ship out of a lawnmower. He became interested in electronics and came to love the graphic language used to describe the flow of electricity between parts.

John majored in English at Middlebury College in Vermont and spent most of his time there hiking and skiing. He was unaware of the field of graphic design, but when he saw a show in the Middlebury library of Leonard Baskin's letterpress broadsides with woodcut illustrations of Robert Frost poems, he knew he wanted to do that too. He got hold of a little proof press and 24-point Century Oldstyle type, and he began setting poems that he had written and printing them along with illustrative woodcuts and etchings.

After college, John explored his adventurous side, teaching primary school in a remote corner of French-Catholic Canada, and also setting sails, rowing, and cutting up, drying, and salting codfish with demonstration teams at the seaport in Mystic, Connecticut. He decided to become an artist and began to study painting, drawing, and printmaking at Wesleyan.

A professor told John, "You might think you're an artist, but you're not. You're a graphic designer," and encouraged him to apply to Yale's graphic design program, which he started in 1979. John's connection to the university has deepened with time. He graduated in 1981, started teaching in 1983, and was named university printer in 1998.

I admire John for knowing how to process fish, for being a secret hippie, for art directing his children's book reports, for being radically conservative, for being a mediocre poet, for loving motorcycles. Most important, I admire him for his point of view about graphic design, about typography, and about teaching.

WWJGD

Unconvinced

John has very strong convictions about graphic design, but he is more open to looking at different types of work than many of the hip young design superstars who visited our program. I think this is because he has a deep skepticism about style and a profound aversion to snobbery. When he started at Yale in 1979, the school was still in the grip of Swiss modernism. There was a sense then that Swiss modernism was what graphic design was. John was unconvinced, believing that graphic design had to be a much broader field, that what his colleagues and teachers were calling graphic design was merely a style within graphic design.

To fight the undertow of style and personal taste, John looks for intentionality in graphic design—visual and conceptual integrity. For him, that is what distinguishes design from art, and distinguishes great design from good design. He also prizes what he calls holography in a piece of design—the sense that as deep as you go, you continue to find new resonances in the work. Typography is the perfect vessel for this interest, in which innumerable design decisions can reinforce a particular approach, providing satisfaction again and again through a kind of layering.

An Oasis from the Madness

A key component of the panic of a graphic design education is the sense of the vastness of the discipline. There are thousands of typefaces, millions of designers, dozens of subfields within design, a constant stream of new media, new platforms, new versions of the Adobe Creative Suite. How can anyone hope to catch up? John's classroom feels like an oasis from the madness.

He finds ways to make graphic design a small world, one that he made seem quite manageable to us. In the first class, he gave a presentation about the history of typography in which he mentioned maybe twenty-five names, and then he referred to them over and over again throughout the course: Gutenberg, Nicholas Jenson, William Caslon, Baskerville, Bodoni, William Morris, Carl Purington Rollins, Bruce Rogers, W. A. Dwiggins, Alvin Eisenman, Joseph Albers, Alvin Lustig, Paul Rand, Brad Thompson, Herbert Matter, Armin Hofmann, Jan Tschichold, Wolfgang Weingart, April Greiman, Sheila deBretteville, Rudy VanderLans, David Carson, Kyle Cooper, Matthew Carter, Tobias Frere-Jones, and Jonathan Hoefler. That was it.

The High Priest

In the foreword to his *Elements of Typographic Style,* Robert Bringhurst defends his choice to write a rulebook for a creative discipline:

> The subject of this book is not typographic solitude, but the old,
> well-traveled roads at the core of the tradition: paths that each of us
> is free to follow or not, and to enter and leave when we choose—if
> only we know the paths are there and have a sense of where they
> lead. That freedom is denied us if the tradition is concealed or left
> for dead. Originality is everywhere, but much originality is blocked
> if the way back to earlier discoveries is cut or overgrown.

If Bringhurst's *Elements* is typography's bible, then John Gambell is its high priest.

John says, "What I teach is not about concepts. They're almost indisputable skills or ways that people have traditionally thought about typographic and design work. They are good to use if you're inclined and certainly good to know if you're not, because they're in effect landmarks in the visual landscape."

In the way of all great Type I classes, we felt like we learned something indisputably true and vitally important in every meeting. In our other classes, in which graphic design could be anything to anyone, we felt rudderless, blind, and victimized by whim. John handed us short documents—often single pages—that simply told us what to do and what not do. John says, "Concentrating on giving people experience with these skills, and in some ways facts, is a good foundation for work. It's less about which formal system you choose than it is about how you create those systems or consciously ignore those systems."

Stop Worrying

When I first taught Type I at California College of the Arts, John's voice was constantly in my head. It said things like, "Provide a practical foundation for people to build out from. . . . Stop worrying about whether people like you. . . . Interrogate the students about what they figure they were doing, and what forces they employ, what they consciously do to make their work what it is. . . . Try to figure out where it is the students want to go and then work with them to make that as strong as it could be."

As I reflect on this person I admire so much, I realize that part of the idea of admiration is that it never ends. It's always aspirational, and as long as you admire someone, you're always looking up to him. I admire John because he teaches and practices the rules of graphic design. Asserting that graphic design has rules might make some people shudder, but for John, the rules are simply truths. They can be rejected, reshaped, or reified, but everything is in their terms. They are like gravity. Or air.

RACHEL BERGER is a graphic designer in Oakland. She works at SYPartners and teaches at California College of the Arts. She holds an MFA from Yale.

"Type is about relationships, continuity, feeling, emotion, movement, and texture. Type is concept too."

—CHERI GRAY
Academy of Art University

"Looking at the development of our writing system since the hieroglyphs, one can witness a gradual simplification of form. It is this simplifying, reducing, and abstracting of information which is one of the main criteria in the language of graphic design."

—FRANZ WERNER
Rhode Island School of Design

"Your long-term success in design will come from three things: perseverance; commitment; and patience, particularly with yourself."

—HANK RICHARDSON
Portfolio Center

"La musica è una continua ispirazione, ascoltala."
"Music is a constant inspiration. Listen to it."

—MARCO CAMPEDELLI
Istituto Design Palladio, Verona, Italy

"Design is hard.*

*especially good design"

—MICHAEL VANDERBYL
California College of the Arts

Elliott Earls interviewed by Kevin Paolozzi

Cranbrook Academy of Art, January 2013

KEVIN: You are the current designer-in-residence of the 2D department at Cranbrook Academy of Art, a unique graduate program in graphic design that encourages an interdisciplinary mode of working. Given the program's unique structure, how does Cranbrook's interdisciplinary model affect the way in which you teach graphic design?

ELLIOTT: It affects absolutely everything about the way that I teach graphic design. The structure of Cranbrook, as you pointed out, is unique, and it lends itself to a certain type of working for the students, and a certain type of teaching or pedagogy for me. Basically what that means is that the academy is very small—there are only 150 students—and most of them live on campus, and the artists-in-residence live in close proximity to their studios. Graduate students are in my studio on a regular basis, and I'm in their studios, but the key component in all of that is that graduate students in 2D or in any discipline at the academy effectively have very intimate relationships with students from other departments: they live with students from other disciplines, they are in very close proximity with students from other disciplines, and they party with students from other disciplines. So on an intellectual, personal, and emotional level, the academy is a very small and intimate community, which lends itself to a kind of internal portability. Ideas that would be happening in, say, the metalsmithing department, or in sculpture, or in 2D, will very quickly find their way into the rest of the ten departments. So on some level, my teaching philosophy and my teaching style are as much a response to the unique structure of Cranbrook as they are a kind of overt shaping on my part.

KEVIN: How would you characterize the work that is coming out of Cranbrook, given that interdisciplinary portability?

ELLIOTT: I think that there is a way of characterizing the work that comes out of the 2D department schematically, and basically, what I mean by that is that if you think of the traditional definitions of graphic design, you think of things like posters, letterheads, logos, corporate communications, signage systems, information architecture, way finding, etc.—those things are ubiquitous. The 2D department begins with those as a kind of starting point, but the department has historically always placed an emphasis on experimental forms of graphic design. Experimental work calls into question the foundational principles of graphic design, the efficiency of communication; it calls into question the role of the designer in the designer/client relationship. So anything that is experimental questions what those relationships are. And then there is also work that is going on in the department that is at a threshold between design and contemporary art.

KEVIN: Can you describe an exhilarating moment that you've experienced as the head of the department?

ELLIOTT: I've had two teaching experiences in my life. Prior to Cranbrook, I taught two classes as an adjunct professor at SUNY Purchase in undergraduate typography. Cranbrook, at the graduate level, I would suggest is an experience that is very exhilarating because of the constant challenges that it poses. The students, at times, can be extremely smart and extremely precocious, so critique on any given Thursday can be extremely intellectually stimulating. The fact that we have a studio and an educational model in place that deals with thinking through making, and the close integration of my students into my work, and me into their work, really makes the whole experience one that is deeply rewarding and deeply stimulating. That is not to suggest that every day is like that; there are days that are filled with meetings and days that are stupefyingly boring, because that is the nature of life. But the overarching experience at Cranbrook has been exhilarating and/or exciting.

KEVIN: How have the teachers you had prior to attaining your role as the department head affected your pedagogy, your teaching methodology?

ELLIOTT: There have been two primary teachers in my life: one is a man named Ron Decker, who is an artist and painter in Covington, Kentucky. When I was about sixteen years old, I started apprenticing with him, going to his brownstone twice a week, and painting, talking about art, and talking about artistic practice. The other main teachers that I have had were the McCoys, who ran the Cranbrook design department from the 1970s to the early 1990s. I was a student under them, and I think that they are brilliant

teachers. They had a very interesting approach to teaching where they were kind of paradoxically hands-off, which I have tried to assimilate, and what I mean by that is that I really believe that mature students, if given a stimulating environment and the right conditions, will naturally excel. It seemed as if their goal was to help foster a really positive, very stimulating environment, so I saw the McCoys more as architects of a more macro condition. The conditions here are very conducive to excellence in education, so I am trying to concern myself with the big picture.

KEVIN: Given the prominence of your own studio practice, what compels you to teach?

ELLIOTT: Before I took the teaching job at Cranbrook, I was not interested in teaching. I taught those courses at SUNY Purchase because, quite frankly, when running my business very early on out of graduate school, I needed the money. I did find it interesting, but I wasn't interested in teaching. What compels me to teach was that I would find myself lecturing at schools all over the United States, and running workshops all over the place in graphic design, and one part of me felt like I had a bunker mentality in relation to the way I was working, wherein I would go back to my studio by myself, work by myself, and felt like I was hiding until the work was done. So when the Cranbrook teaching job became available, I knew how amazing the Cranbrook environment was, and I was definitely interested in that. I was also interested in challenging myself to understand the universal principle that I believe in—that I am strengthened by helping other people, and that I am in fact strengthened by being open, and helping other people to grow, that I am not diminished.

KEVIN: What would you characterize as the most important thing to take away from graduate study in graphic design?

ELLIOTT: A perfect example is that for our reading group, I am working with William Pistner, who is one of the teachers at Cranbrook Kingswood, an excellent boarding high school here in the Cranbrook Educational Community. We are reading Henry David Thoreau's *Walden*. The most important component of being a good designer is immersing oneself in the humanities—those things that make us deeply human. So, as an example, we are not reading some text written by a graphic designer—we are reading philosophy. The idea that you

are supposed to take away from the educational experience is that the thing that makes you a good designer is a rich life, and rich sources to draw on. You go to the source; you go to deep texts to do that. But not only deep texts: good films, good music, good literature. The kind of surface treatment is not important.

ELLIOTT EARLS *is the designer-in-residence and head of the graduate program in 2D design at Cranbrook Academy of Art.*

KEVIN PAOLOZZI *is a graphic designer based out of Toronto, Canada. He holds a master of design degree in graphic design from York University, and a master of fine arts degree in 2D design from Cranbrook Academy of Art.*

"QUESTION THE PREMISE."

—PATRICK FITZGERALD
North Carolina State University
College of Design

"If it is not helping you, it is hurting you. It is either doing something good for you or it is a competitive distraction."

—LOU DANZIGER
Art Center College of Design

"The one thing I'm constantly saying to my students is, 'Why?' They say, 'I'm going to do the type in brown,' and I say, 'Why?' And they have to go away until they can give me a good answer."

—MARIKO JESSE
Central Saint Martins, London

"Be a fearless designer. It's the client's job to have fear."

—MARANATHA WILSON
Minneapolis College of Art and Design

"PLAY!"

—**HANK RICHARDSON**

Portfolio Center

"I entered the CCAC graphic design program in 1993 and had the good fortune of having Steve Reoutt as one of my first instructors. For Steve, the discipline of working steadily and making progress every day was more important than the 'success' of our final work. Steve made us sketch in large pads of newsprint every day, whether we felt like it or not. At the end of every assignment, he would take the time to meet with us individually to go through our newsprint pad.

During one of his reviews of my sketchpad, he looked at me and said, 'You're a good problem solver, and you work hard. I know form making doesn't come easily for you, but no one has it all. Work hard, and the rest will come in time.'

His faith—and the rigor of his approach—had a profound impact on me as a student. It encouraged me to be patient, and it allowed me to grow as a designer at my own pace. I have been teaching Typography 1 in the graphic design program at CCA for seven years now, and, like Steve, I collect and review my students' process sketches at the end of every assignment."

—ANGIE WANG
California College of the Arts

Greerisms :: *by John Gambell*

Greer Allen had a terrific lecture, first presented at the University of Virginia, that was intriguingly titled "All I Know About Book Design I Learned on the Race-track." Paraphrasing that, I can say: "All I know about working as a designer—and a lot more than that too—I learned from Greer Allen." Here are a few of those lessons.

LESSON ONE: "PLAN AHEAD."

I don't remember just the occasion, but I was troubling Greer for advice as I very often did. I asked him how I should go about giving a brief public presentation on a design-related subject. His response went something like this:

"Good God, John, they don't want to listen to you fumbling around for the right word, or losing your way halfway through your talk. Write down what you plan to say ahead of time, then *read* it to them—with *emphasis!*"

I've followed his advice for the most part ever since, and I have found that taking the trouble to plan my work and presentations, to put my thoughts into writing—which I'm much better at than speaking—has served me well.

LESSON TWO: "DESIGN BY LISTENING."

Shortly after I started working for Greer at the Yale Printing Service, I had a tussle with a client who was concerned that my work did not reflect his hopes for the printed piece.

Much of my schooling had seemed to focus upon sticking to design principles, and among my teachers had been towering authority figures such as Paul Rand and Armin Hofmann.

As I took on projects, I could often envision a finished design, so why, for heaven's sake, didn't this client see it *my* way, too, or at least defer to my schooled expertise?

Greer wasn't especially sympathetic with my frustration, and he said, "John, I design by listening. I really listen to my clients." He went on to add that on a number of occasions he had been "saved by a client" from making regrettable design choices. This ran counter to my sense of graphic designers as self-directed artistic heroes.

Greer sincerely wanted each of his projects to reflect his client's intentions. He labored to make what his clients *would* make if they had a designer's talents and training. This posture was at the heart of Greer's design practice and was first dramatized for me when he asked me to help him with some administrative chores connected with the Yale University Art Gallery's John Trumbull catalogue in 1981.

Greer said that a file I needed for the job could be found in a box on his desk. I returned to him saying that I hadn't been able to find a Trumbull or Art Gallery folder in that location. A little surprised, he said, "John, the material's right there, in the folder marked 'Helen.'"

Helen Cooper was his client contact and the curator of that important project.

Greer's filing system was a revelation. His projects were as much or more about *who* he was working with as about *what* he was working on. Thus I began to understand design by listening.

LESSON THREE: "GET ON WITH IT."

After I started working at the Yale University Printing Service, I came to feel very much at ease with Greer. He was always a wise, if not always entirely patient, listener.

Toward the end of one day, I spoke with Greer at unusual length (both of us standing near his desk, of course) about how I was wrestling with the concerns that trouble a young designer—about the difficulties of balancing work with the demands of child care, and so on. When I had finally run through my list of confessions and complaints, about which Greer was warmly helpful, he smiled mischievously and said, "John, it's clear that you are a tangle of complexes, but now you've simply got to get on with it."

I laughed, and got on with it.

The formal, technical, and financial challenges, the client relationships, and the ever-changing content of commissions delighted and diverted Greer. For him, the work of design or printing—the work of the day—took precedence over *talk*, however congenial that talk might be.

"Follow me," Greer would say if I approached him with a question that he feared would take some time to discuss. He would literally lope around the shop multitasking—I'd be a few feet behind, chattering away, working to get his full attention. During these traveling conversations, Greer would review jobs or investigate technical glitches, or whatever, while he carried on with his tag-along colleague.

On days when I struggle to stick to my to-do list, I hear Greer's mischievous and wise, "John, get on with it!"

"Plan ahead," "design by listening," "get on with it." These are three "Greerisms" I took to heart while working for him—all of them imprinted on me by his exuberant, positive personality. These have been valuable lessons, and when I have succeeded in my work, it has largely been on their account.

JOHN GAMBELL teaches typography at Yale School of Art and currently serves as Yale's institutional art director with the grand but misleading title of University Printer.

"Critique is an opportunity for growth, both as a designer and as a person."

—BRAD BARTLETT
Art Center College of Design

"Processes are more interesting than ideas.

The point being to not stare at the ceiling hoping for divine intervention."

—RODERICK GRANT
OCAD University, Toronto, ON

"Students need to engage in research for every project inside and outside of the classroom. Providing a written record of procedures and conclusions will be of benefit to all involved, teachers, students, and community partners as well to a wider audience."

—MAY CHUNG
NSCAD University, Halifax, NS

—WALTER JUNGKIND
Professor Emeritus, University of Alberta, Edmonton, AB

"IF YOU CAN'T JOIN THE CLUB, CREATE ONE."

—LINDSAY NOHL
Minneapolis College of Art and Design

"One of the mantras I keep repeating to my graphic design students is, 'White space is important!' as most of the time only content gets the deserved attention, leaving the blank parts as leftovers."

—MARTA BERNSTEIN
Politecnico di Milano, Milan, Italy

KT Meaney interviewed by Tina Hardison

TINA: What was your path to becoming a design educator?

KT: "How often I found where I should be going only by setting out for somewhere else." —*Buckminster Fuller*

I was a painting major initially, and I took a typography course taught by John Sherman who, through content and charisma, changed the trajectory of my life.

TINA: Did you have a single moment when you knew you wanted to teach?

KT: Like many people, I just fell into it. The moment I questioned my decision to teach was at the School of Visual Arts during a "How To" on how not to cut yourself with an X-Acto knife. It didn't end well.

Don't gesticulate with a sharp object in one hand.

TINA: Did you have any design teachers or mentors that largely influenced you? Any memorable take-aways from them?

KT: Tracey Cameron, associate, Pentagram Design. Perfect the art of storytelling; it is the perfect aid to (delivery system for) teaching.

and

Michael Bierut, partner, Pentagram Design.

I call myself a "Pentagrad," because working on Michael's team was a design education.

Seduce the client with near-final first-round proposals.

TINA: What do you feel is the most important thing for students to take away from your classes?

KT: I believe in Fartlek conditioning. Fartlek is a method of exercise that interrupts continuous training with variation in pace. A lengthy run, say, would be punctuated by well-earned walks. I've discovered that variation in activities, processes, and time frames is more engaging than continuous output. Assignments that force a student to sit in front of a computer screen for hours are unhealthy. I want my students to stay in motion.

The more you move, the better you think.

TINA: Let's hear some of your KT Meaney "designisms."

KT: Don't wait for a good idea. Find a good idea. You can force this by doing such things as browsing the library, taking a shower, hiking, talking over an idea with peers, or purposely making something bad.

Avoid dorm-room design (this is design that is too congested for its space).

TINA: Describe one of your most exhilarating classroom moments.

KT: There is magic in graphic design: Two colors overprinted can give the illusion of three. An arrow forces one to gaze in a particular direction. Still frames animate in our minds through the principle of closure.

Type students at North Carolina State University design a publication in their junior year. The brief requires integration of type and image. The imagery part is always problematic: underconsidered, visually meaningless, cognitively devoid, and often low res.

Only one student in my four years
of teaching the assignment actually
staged a photo shoot that related to
her text. She constructed buildings
out of cardboard. She combined these
models with flat photographic elements and dimensional line art. She
did this all on her own.

Instead of trying to find an image that
worked, she worked her image to fit the
content. And her type design was high
level too.

When a student delivers something
inventive and beyond expectations,
there is magic in teaching.

TINA HARDISON *is an East–to-West-Coast
transplant, having attended the College of
Design at North Carolina State University. Tina
is a past Chronicle Books designer, and she is
currently an iBooks designer at Apple and communications co-chair for AIGA San Francisco.*

KATHLEEN (KT) MEANEY *has taught at the
School of Visual Arts in New York City, the
College of Design at North Carolina State
University, and is currently at the University
of Illinois, Champaign-Urbana. Her research
explores the potential of the digital humanities in the realm of exhibit design.*

"Don't use defaults; make decisions. (No auto leading. Only use a 1-point rule if you have chosen that weight.)"

—LESLIE FRIESEN
Hite Art Institute,
University of Louisville

"The 'Three Twos' Rule: Every piece of design needs to work in two seconds, two minutes, and two hours. This is actually something I heard from my friend, the designer Jean Orlebeke. It's a reminder that the simplest projects can still have depth, and the complicated ones still need to engage audiences in visceral, direct ways."

—ERIC HEIMAN
California College of the Arts

"Method is more important than style. Style lives fast and dies young."

—BRAD BARTLETT
Art Center College of Design

"If the scope of a project is overwhelming and paralyzing, find a small part that doesn't scare you and start there; then the next small part, etc. [Partial inspiration from Anne Lamott's *Bird by Bird: Some Instruction on Writing and Life*.]"

—MARTHA SCOTFORD
North Carolina State University
College of Design

"Go big and risk screwing up now. Your life will be full of other opportunities to be acceptable."

—ANDREW SLOAT
Rhode Island School of Design

Sweat Equity :: *by Natalie Davis*

My best days as a teacher happen when I don't need to say much. They are the days when students make breakthroughs with their work or vocalize a critique with the perfect tone and thoughtfulness. They are the days when I am no longer needed, and the students move forward on their own. They have absorbed and learned to ask the right questions, to trust themselves, and to be fearless. It takes work and long hours to reach that point, but you can get there with perseverance and a bit of advice. Your best days as a designer are straight ahead.

ON INSPIRATION

Stay focused. Don't always look to trendy social media sites for "inspiration" or "research." There is a time and place for research in the design process, but many students use it as a crutch to lean on when they hit a brick wall. Instead of doing the hard work, they procrastinate and do research, which often isn't effective. Unfortunately, students are looking at the same websites and being inspired by the same people, so projects start to feel derivative and watered down. It's disheartening to watch students copy other designers. Seek your inspiration in unexpected places. Expand beyond the web for research, and get out in the world—to a bookstore, library, or theater. Follow other passions that you may have put aside too soon. Read a science textbook or browse *Psychology Today* at your local bookstore. Go to the ballet, borrow your younger sister's graphic novels, and volunteer at a food bank. Take a road trip and bring along a camera and your sketchbook. Expand your life experiences and the circle of people you interact with day to day, and your work will become richer and deeper in meaning.

ON HARD WORK

Fail hard. Fail often. Keep trying. Students give up very easily and struggle when things don't come quickly. Instead of trying to work through a problem, they throw their hands up and yell, "I can't do it. This is terrible!" They get frustrated because they can't physically manifest what they visualize in their minds. But if you just put your head down and work through it, kicking and fighting yourself if needed, you will finish the project and learn something from it. Maybe the result is not exactly what you envisioned, but you are much closer to that vision now than when you first started. The next time you tackle a similar problem, you will be better equipped. As you start to master your tools and trust your own instincts, all the time and effort put into your work will show. Accept that it will take time to get there, and it only happens through working hard. There is no substitute for that. Not even raw talent will survive without hard work.

As you first venture into design, you are like a toddler learning to walk. Professors will show you tools and talk about color, composition, type, and movement, demanding that you consider all of this while taking your first steps. You will fall, creating awkward layouts without enough margins. You will fall again, setting body text in display typefaces that aren't legible when printed. You will keep falling over and over until you are exhausted, with projects that make the eye dizzy or that bore. And that's exactly when you have to get yourself up and try again. Expect to fall repeatedly in the beginning: it does not mean you are a bad designer, or that you have no hope or potential. It means that you are trying, and you have to keep trying, no matter what.

As time goes on and you gain more experience, your work will slowly improve. Let's pause right here in this book. I'd like you to find a sketchbook from a few years ago, maybe from high school or your freshman year of college. If those are packed away, open up a folder on your computer with projects from years ago. Take some time to remember what the assignment was and what you were trying to achieve with the piece. Painful, right? Now look at your work today. Huge improvements! In a few years, you'll look at the work you're making today and react with the same cringe. That's how we know we're learning.

The key to understanding design is that it is a process, one that takes time to work through. Students look at finished projects on portfolio websites and fail to see the work behind it—all of the thumbnails, drafts, revisions, teardowns, and re-dos that helped a designer reach that final piece. Finished projects take time. You can be certain that a beautiful, portfolio-worthy piece is not what was presented to the class at a final critique. By the time it makes it into a portfolio, the project has been reworked and polished many times over. The designers may have had to start the process all over again, after realizing where they got off track or missed an opportunity. Few projects ever feel truly done, but by understanding the process and working through all the stages of design, you can arrive at a solution worth sharing.

Expect *more* from yourself. You are capable of truly amazing work, but if you don't expect that from yourself, it will never happen. Professors can push you, your classmates can push you, but in the end, you have to push yourself. Any success I've had in my life started with an internal drive to make something better. This drive pushes me to have wild, crazy dreams of doing something new, to get excited at the potential before me, and to make opportunities where none existed before. That begins by expecting great things from yourself and making them happen by sheer willpower and hard work. Sometimes that means suspending disbelief, from yourself and others, but if you truly believe in it—I mean down-in-your-bones believe it—then you can make it happen.

ON CREATIVE BLOCKS

The big lesson is that it takes work—consistent work—to be good. You have to fail a lot and often, and you have to pick yourself back up off the studio floor when things don't go your way. When students are struggling, I'll often tell them to go take a walk. Get out of their heads, stop forcing it, and take a mental and physical break. Often the solution comes to us when we are not thinking about it consciously. One of the best product ideas I've ever had came to me while I was doing dishes. With my hands submerged in soapy water and my mind wandering, I was able to untangle a problem that had been bothering me for a few days. (I can't guarantee that washing dishes will solve your design problems, but at the very least, you will have clean dishes.) Being creative on demand doesn't always work, so we need to give ourselves space and time to let ideas brew for a bit. That also means we have to stick to a strict schedule to allow for the daydreaming process. You won't have time to let an idea breathe if you've been procrastinating.

ON CRITIQUE

Smile, stay positive, and listen with an open mind to the feedback you are given during critique. It is intended to help move you forward, not tear you down. It is *not* personal. It's advice given to improve your work, and it allows you the chance to do that. Be grateful for the time and attention folks are giving to your work. Learn to relish it and incorporate the suggestions in your revisions. Critique is magic! You get what you give during crit, so be sure to pay attention and share your ideas. Nothing is worse than presenting work and receiving no response from the audience. Learn how to address the difficulties in another student's work, and you will find that it helps your work as well. Take notes during critique, because you are probably struggling with the same issues as the person presenting, and oftentimes a solution or suggestion will come up that also applies to you.

One thing I remind my students is that we are all in this together. I have been in their shoes. I have been nervous before a critique or scared of what someone will think about my work. Everyone is scared, and that's OK. Acknowledge the feeling, but don't let it cripple you. The trick we've all heard again and again is to "fake it 'til you make it." It works! Fake your confidence during a presentation, and soon enough you really gain it.

The first class I taught was an extended education course on typography for professionals. I had students who had been designing for longer than I had been out of college. My hands nervously shook as I drew letterforms on the board. But I kept an even tone to my voice, stayed calm, and faked the confidence I wish I felt at the time. I thought of all the professors I had admired at school and what they did in front of their classes. I relied on my theater experience to act out a role, and then I grew into it. Years later, I am that calm professor who can manage a classroom of seasoned professionals or nervous freshmen.

ON ENTERING THE REAL WORLD

When making the transition from school to working as a designer, there is no magical transformation that happens when you get a diploma. The working habits you have as a student are the same ones you will have in the real world. If you constantly procrastinate, that won't change when you have a deadline from a client versus a deadline from a professor. Pay attention to how you work now, and take notes on the process. It's important to spend time reflecting on finished projects and find ways you could have improved and remember ways in which you succeeded. It takes us all a while before we know which methods work best for us.

Care about the work you are doing right now. If you don't take your schoolwork seriously, then school might not be the best place for you now. Respect that the work you are creating is what will ultimately go into your portfolio, and treat it as such. These are the projects that will get you noticed and hired. It may not always seem obvious to you, but class assignments have important goals that build your repertoire as a designer. If you don't take your work seriously, how can you expect anyone else to take you seriously as a designer?

ON FEARS

Don't be scared to ask questions and interact with your professors. It may seem intimidating, but they are there to help you. Design professors are a wealth of knowledge about lots of different things, not just graphic design. Find one that you connect with, and share your work. Ask for feedback, talk about your design passions, and ask about their journeys. Everyone has a unique path, and you never know what interesting stops people may have made along the way. You'll find that in our field, there is no such thing as a traditional career path, and it's reassuring to learn the many different needs for design in the world, especially those outside of a traditional studio or agency experience. Get to know your professors as real people, and be supportive of their research interests. You never know when an opportunity might present itself for an internship. I often recommend my students for work, but not if I don't know them well.

Learn to trust yourself as a designer and a person. It's important to listen to feedback, but first you must decide what to do. You cannot be driven by fear into making decisions that you don't really support. Quiet the noise around you, and ask yourself, "What's the concept? Which solution will support that idea?" Stop asking others to make decisions for you, because design by committee does not work. The buck stops with you, and the sooner you take responsibility for your work, the stronger it will be.

ON TYPE

Type is the foundation of graphic design. Students often run away from type, fearing it like the bogeyman. If you run away from type in school, you will run away from it your entire career. Your portfolio will show it, and you won't get very far with your work.

Immerse yourself in type at school and you will be ahead of the crowd. Nerd out on letter anatomy, pay attention to the details, and start drawing letters for practice. Start with the classics, tracing curves and terminals. The more you draw type, the more you will train your eye to see the differences among letterforms. It's valuable to learn type history and understand how and why letterforms developed to reflect changes in society. That rich background will make it easier for you to select the right typeface among thousands for your project. Just like people, typefaces have their own baggage, so spend time with them to understand why they act the way they do.

NATALIE DAVIS is a graphic designer and assistant professor at Texas State San Marcos. She received her BA in design/media arts from UCLA and her MFA in 2D design from Cranbrook.

"We're in the business of inspiring and fostering, not persuading."

—AMBER HOWARD
North Carolina State University
College of Design

"I hope that you at least take away from [my class] one or two fragments of knowledge that you can attribute to the hard work you put in under my guidance (perhaps if both you and I were doing our job right, they will be more than fragments and in greater quantity). Even the trivia (like the fact that John Baskerville was buried vertically, standing up) can come in handy someday (?). . . . Remember that design is an honorable, stimulating, and rewarding discipline, field, and craft. It *is* important. You are shaping, ordering, and making interesting communication and information that will touch countless people. You are solving problems that only a handful can solve—and of that handful, you are the only one with your solution. Even the smallest message deserves your mindful and complete attention. If no one tells you that again, in school or in the 'real world,' know that it is true."

—JOHN V. CLARKE
University of Dayton

"STAY AWAKE. The first five years after graduation are important to laying down the foundation of a fulfilling career. Stay awake and live them with intention."

—MELANIE DOHERTY
California College of the Arts

"The best inspiration comes from unexpected sources. Let life inspire your designs."

—JASON DUBIN
Art Center College of Design

"GO BACK TO THE IDEA."

—ANDY PRESSMAN
Parsons The New School for Design

"Bisogna ritornare a guardare il cielo."

"We must go back and look at the sky."

—MARCO CAMPEDELLI
Istituto Design Palladio, Verona, Italy

Douglass Scott interviewed by Benjamin Shaykin

BEN: How did you begin teaching graphic design?

DOUG: The first class I ever taught was when I was a graduate student at Yale. It was a general graphic design course for nonmajors. For students in the drama school.

BEN: The drama school?

DOUG: Yes. It was for people who were going to be theater administrators. The dean of the school thought it would be valuable for those students to learn what designers do, because they would be dealing with designers for the rest of their lives.

BEN: Interesting. So it was a way for them to understand the language?

DOUG: Yes. And so I gave them basic information about printing, typography. I had them do a couple of theater posters, because I thought that would help them to think about symbolism. That was the first class I taught. That was 1973.

And then, when I left Yale and came to Boston, I started teaching at the Boston Architectural Center. I had some ideas about what I wanted to teach. I taught basic design, I taught color, I taught graphic design, and I taught a quasi architecture/graphic design course where we did signage and things for buildings. And I remember trying to figure out: How do teachers do this job? I had some things I wanted to get across, and I invented projects. Some of those were somewhat like assignments that I had gotten as a student—either in architecture at Nebraska or at Yale—and other times, I was just making up stuff. But the big thing I learned in those early years was how to have a personal relationship with a student so that you got him or her to do what you wanted. That's the part that nobody ever talked about. It's a personality thing, as you know. The goal is to foster a mutual respect.

And at this same time, Chris Pullman [Doug's boss at WGBH] invited me to come to Yale with him, because his classes were getting so large he couldn't make it around the room in one day. He needed help, so he invited me to come work with him. He had been my teacher, so I knew how he operated. I remember

Chris would sometimes put me on the difficult people, because I liked to talk to them. I would just try to convince them that this was a valuable experience.

It was valuable for me as well, because I could watch Chris teach again, and I admired his teaching greatly. And then in 1980, my sixth year of working professionally, Tom Ockerse called and said, "I need somebody to teach graphic design history." RISD had never had it before. And this was the time when people were starting to get interested in this. Lou Danziger and Phil Meggs had been teaching history, and Keith Godard in Philadelphia, but very few knew about them. It was only in small circles.

When Tom asked me if I would come teach history, I had actually been preparing to do this in Boston. I was going to find a school in Boston . . .

BEN: But you hadn't done it yet?

DOUG: I had made over 2,000 slides. I was ready to go, just about, when he called me. I said yes, I could do it, because I was prepared. That was thirty-three years ago.

BEN: And so history of graphic design was the first class you taught at RISD?

DOUG: Yes. This was when all of a sudden, the RISD undergrad program exploded in size. The department got twice as big, and that's when so many professors came: Aki [Nurosi], Hammett [Nurosi], me, Jan Baker, a couple of others. We all came at about the same time.

BEN: Did the history class have a studio component from the start, or did that develop later?

DOUG: I had people write a paper the first year, and then I realized, because of the RISD student mentality, that that was not going to fly. They told me right off the bat. They said, "We have to do this for our art history classes. And we hate this."

At that time it was an elective for seniors, so I had twelve or fifteen people. I started by having them write an essay, but we made them into little booklets or accordions. And then it became an illustrated essay. And then from there, over the years, it became a poster. Then it became two projects: a poster about a design landmark and an accordion timeline about a designer, which I think works pretty well, because the two different forms are good research, writing, and design assignments.

BEN: Would you say you experiment with different assignments until you find the one that works?

DOUG: Yes, until I find something that I think works well. But of course, things change; the profession is changing. The students change; the schools change. Other people might do something in another class, so I feel like I don't need to do that any more, because someone else is handling it.

I'm constantly changing the projects, even if I have been working with one for a while. Such as this year, in exhibit design, I went back to a team project, because in talking to the students last year, the team projects they had done in their other classes had not been very successful. And I thought, well wait a minute—when you go out to work, it's all about the team. So I thought it would be good to try it again.

BEN: What are some examples of things you've seen in other classes that have made you change what you're doing?

DOUG: I will tell you, for Grad Type III this year . . . I had helped a bunch of grad students put their portfolios together last year, and I was stunned that they didn't have any identity work. I thought, "Well, why don't you?" And they said, "We never had the opportunity." Because the only opportunity they would have had was to take the one brand-identity class, but none of them had, because of scheduling constraints. I had been doing an identity project in my undergraduate Type 3, but I had always opted for a more theoretical approach for the grads.

And so I said, "I've got to add an identity project, because it does make sense for typography. It's system oriented." So I tried it this year, and I had to make other projects smaller, which is often good. Sometimes the projects get to be so big and complicated that you can't see the reason for them anymore.

BEN: We've touched on this a little bit, the difference between the undergraduates and graduates, and how you approach them in a more or less theoretical way. Do you feel like there are easy distinctions to make? Are

there differences in your philosophy or what you feel they need to get out of the program?

DOUG: I think ultimately you're teaching the same thing. Essentially, you're teaching people a bunch of skills that they can use, and *a process by which they use those skills*—so that with the skills and the process that they have developed, they can solve any problem they encounter.

I think with the digital technologies that have changed design so much, eventually these students will have to fall back on some pretty basic things: the skills and the process. So you test for those things. And sometimes you make the test complicated. Sometimes you make it simple. Sometimes you leave it open so that they can use various media to solve the problem, or you make it simple and small, knowing that they will be able to make the jump from that simple 11-by-17-inch poster to something bigger.

I think that's true for grads and undergrads. The grad students often have not had the right training early enough to help them make effortless work, I think. I have seen over the years that the grad students are often really challenged in areas that are pretty basic: form, color, adaptability. I would also say *fearlessness*. The undergrads have a fearless approach, probably due to their foundation courses. They don't seem daunted. And they have an openness to solving things differently, or using media that they're not familiar with. I think the grads are often cautious. They usually have come to graphic design from other areas of study, so they haven't had the formal training. You don't see many grad students in graphic design that have come from painting, or areas where they've had a really good foundation that allows them to find different media or to mix things in different ways.

But the other thing that's going on with the graduates is that they are intellectually more open to many things and have experienced much. You can really use the experience and knowledge they have. And ultimately, I think that's one of the nice things about grad students—the teachers become involved in the intellectual pursuit at a higher level than with the undergrads.

Of course, I don't want to say all grads are that way, because you always have grad students who are extremely good at form, or have had so much experience that their process is good, because

they've been working professionally in a way where one has had to solve all kinds of problems. But it is true that the grad students have the capacity, interest, and a yen for high-level thinking, for theoretical issues, that undergrads usually aren't that interested in yet. And that makes the work richer.

BEN: When you have a class like Exhibit Design, which you've been doing for a long time, you have both grads and undergrads in the same class. How do you . . .

DOUG: There it's a different problem, and the world of three-dimensional work is daunting. And difficult. I'm told to take twelve people, so I take twelve graphic designers. But I can handle eighteen with a teacher's assistant. So I will pick six people from other departments: architecture, industrial design, interior architecture. I've had some people from glass; I've had some people from furniture. So most of those people, all of them actually, are three-dimensional thinkers. And that has been great for everybody.

BEN: You studied architecture in undergrad, yes?

DOUG: Yes, I was in a BArch program at the University of Nebraska. They are starting to disappear. A BArch program means you go in as a freshman and you are thrust into the cold water of architecture for five years.

Most of your time is immersed in architecture. In that way, you have that old tradeschool, or beaux arts, education, where you're just consumed by it. And because you're dealing with engineering, you have to take calculus and physics. And then you get into engineering mechanics, and then you get into structure: wood, concrete, steel.

And so you're moving through a design world, but it's supported by engineering, structure, and then these other little things you take at the beginning: English, math. That's just to make sure that you can deal with those things. But everything else goes away. It's a brutal education. You're working all night, and you're just barely getting to your other classes. And I loved it.

When I was in school, people didn't get really serious until their third year out of the five. I'm aware of this in my own students here. The first two years are adapting to college life. Particularly at a big university, where there is so much going on.

And you're still questioning whether you really want to do what you're doing. But by the end of the second year, you think, "Okay, I love this and I want to do this well." And so I immediately jumped, I think, from the middle of the pack to the elite in design. And there were a bunch of us for whom that was our life: design. And that's when you suddenly realize, well, design can change the world, and that's what we were being taught. And you put all your energy into architecture studio classes.

BEN: And what led you to graphic design?

DOUG: In my third year of architecture school, some friends in the dormitory came to me and said, "Would you like to design a set for our play?" And I of course said yes. And that was because architecture training makes you think you can do anything. And then they said, "Will you design the poster for the show?" I said, "Sure." But I had never designed a poster before. And then, "Will you do the program?" I was immediately thrust into the world of graphic design, and I loved it.

And so I think it was late in my third year that I realized there was a guy teaching commercial art in the art department, Keith Jacobshagen. He was a painter and photographer; that's what he did professionally. But because he was the youngest faculty member, he had to teach the one commercial art class that they had to offer. So I went over there and said I'm interested in this. I want to know more. I got to know him really well. And I took the class with the art students and found out I loved this. We did a book cover. We did a poster. We did the logo for a magazine. It was fun.

I became the art director of the yearbook. I saw it as an opportunity to learn book design. I was still doing architecture, but now I was taking every advantage I could to learn about graphic design, what it is.

BEN: **Still as a student?**

DOUG: As a student. I was doing a lot of work on campus. I became the designer for the student activities offices. I did a poster once every two weeks. Sometimes big university calendars. And I

began to brush up against the graphic design world. That's why I began to feel pulled away from architecture.

BEN: **Did your experience in architecture school influence your teaching?**

DOUG: Well, here's another thing about teachers: Teachers end up doing the things that were done to them. You can always fall back and say, when I was in so-and-so's class, we did this, and I got this out of it. So that seemed like a pretty good thing. I never wanted to copy exactly what was done to me. So I would always try to adapt the project so it was more me, although the underpinnings might have been some other thing I had done in the past.

And that's why it's important to me to sit down early—I've done this for myself and also when helping younger teachers—and say, what do you want people to learn this semester? And if you write down what you want them to learn, then you figure out, OK, what kind of project can I give them that will let them learn that? Not that I'm going to teach it that way—sometimes you have to give information; sometimes people have to do it themselves.

So you say, this is what I want them to learn, this is the project I'm going to give them so they can experience that, this is what they're going to end up with. And then at the end of the project, you go back and talk about whatever you learned. And so the big question is, are there variables? How long should it take, and how big is the thing?

I always thought back to the teachers I had—what was the goal of our projects? What were we supposed to learn? Sometimes you think, "We spent too much time doing this. This could be a much simpler thing." But sometimes the teacher lost control.

And I do want control of this situation. I don't want to give up the control of what happens during class. But I feel like I'm always open for things to happen that you weren't sure about.

BEN: Like what? What's a good example?

DOUG: Well, you set up a situation and you know what the goal is, but somehow you make the playing field big enough so that maybe you don't get to where you had intended, but you get somewhere else. You've given people enough room to go somewhere else. And sometimes people will end up where you didn't expect, but somehow you set up the parameters so that it has an acceptable ending.

Sometimes you can say, "I want you to make a presentation on blah, blah, blah." And then the students have to figure out, "What am I going to do? Am I going to make a book?" There's more openness, which they can see is a good thing.

That's why I always like to teach sophomores, juniors, seniors, *and* grads, because then you experience the full range of what the possibilities are. With the sophomores, you rein them in a little bit. The grads—you don't have to rein it in so much. You have to encourage them to expand.

BEN: That makes total sense. I feel like the way you write your syllabi, and the way you organize and structure your classes, is like nothing else I've seen. Is that a similar sort of programmatic thinking?

DOUG: I think that a syllabus should clearly state the project parameters, a visual schedule of the semester, and what the students will learn. Also, a list of resources.

And I will tell you . . . recently, I have seen syllabi from other teachers. And I read them and I think they are the most verbose things I have ever seen. There's just way too many words. Because I think often it's a pretty simple thing that we're asking students to do. And I don't want them to be overwhelmed. I have found that when people read those verbose ones, they're often confused as to what they're doing and why.

But I also question my own approach sometimes. I think, "Is this project too small, and clear enough? Or too organized?" As long as I can say, "This is what we're going to do, and this is how much time it's going to take, and this is what you're going to end up with," then it's up to me to be the personal contact. During the process, I am always there: watching, evaluating, giving advice, saying "I don't think you're going in the right direction." There's a symbiotic relationship between how you are during the process as a human being dealing with these people and what the intended goal is that you set up in the beginning.

The physical space also has a lot to do with it. If the classroom is too small, that's a problem. I like moving furniture around to accommodate what we do. I think it's also important for people to get up and walk around during our five-hour studios.

The other problem that all the teachers have is, how do you challenge both the people who go really fast and get there quickly, and the people who are more methodical, slower workers? Or those who have difficulty understanding? And you need to figure out how to balance that so that everybody has a good experience at the time. I also like to have the students doing four or five activities in a long five-hour studio: crits, evaluating good models, helping others, etc.

What it comes down to is you have to have a perception of each student in the time and space, and with their skill level, and hope that you can give them what they need.

BEN: **How do you share your own work?**

DOUG: I bring examples or slides of my work to class. In the '90s, I guess it was '95, I was invited to have a retrospective of my work at the Montserrat School, just north of Boston. They gave me a huge space. And it was good for me, because I had to organize my work. And I had to talk. I gave two talks: a public one when it opened and a gallery talk later on.

This is a good thing for all designers to do. You have to show slides and say, "What have I been doing with my life?"

BEN: **But not in a bad, existential way?**

DOUG: No, it was good! Because it makes you think: What do I value? And you also see threads in your work that you don't usually see, because you can't stand far enough away.

BEN: **And you started teaching directly out of school?**

DOUG: I did.

BEN: **Was that your intention, or did you stumble into it?**

DOUG: I had flirted with the idea of leaving Yale and going back to the Midwest and teaching in a university. But on second thought, I realized I wasn't that interested in that.

BEN: **Because you didn't want to be a full-time teacher, or because you didn't want to be back in the Midwest?**

DOUG: I didn't even know what a full-time teacher did. And I wanted to work. And then when Pullman said, "Do you want to come work for me [at WGBH]?" I said, "Yeah. I do." And I was only going to work there for a year.

BEN: **Right. And you worked with him for . . . ?**

DOUG: Thirty-five years. Because the work changed constantly. Pullman was a very inspirational guy. And he valued teaching, because it was part of his life. He was this great model for me. When I went to him and said, "Can I teach at RISD once a week?" he said, "Sure. You just have to make up the time."

BEN: **And that brings up the idea of a teaching lineage. It's something you and I have talked about a little bit in the past. Do you think about that? Your lineage and who you learned from and who they learned from, and your students who have gone on to teach . . . ?**

DOUG: Well, in architecture, I was aware. We were always aware of where these teachers studied, who their heroes were.

BEN: And for you, would you say that the teacher you looked to was Chris Pullman, or were there other teachers? Obviously, he was a big influence on you.

DOUG: I will tell you, every teacher I had at Yale had a huge influence on me. But I had already had a huge influence from a lot of my teachers from Nebraska. I was always very aware of what they were giving me, how they fit into the whole.

BEN: One of the things we've talked about before is the idea of being very conscious of what you're learning. At the end of a project, or the end of a class, you always ask students, "What did we learn from this?" Where did that come from?

DOUG: I think it came from my own desire to know why we were doing stuff. It's easy to fall into *not* talking about it. In architecture training, you talk about and defend everything you do: why you chose the material, why there were six steps and not eight. Little things like that. And you have to really *think*. But that's why things in architecture often

get to be confrontational— because people are nitpicking you. And so I learned pretty quickly to talk about the big idea, the conceptual idea of why the building is the way it is. And then later on, you learn that all these details feed into the big idea. Which I think is clearly true about graphic design.

BEN: Do you feel like you could articulate your approach to critique?

DOUG: I try to go along with the students' point of view and build on their ideas. But there's logic involved. You can tell students the hierarchy doesn't work. Or that there's not enough leading. But that, again, might be taste, or not. You could bring it up and say, "If I were you, I would put in more leading."

BEN: More leading? Just in general?

DOUG: Well, people make things too tight.

BEN: How do you get students to talk about their own work, and how do you get students to talk about each other's work?

DOUG: Well, the easiest thing to say is, "Look at this person's work, and I want you to find the three things that you think would make it better." That way people can articulate it. They might say that the pictures are too big or too small. Or that there's not enough color; it's kind of dull looking. And if they can say that, that's good. At least they're thinking. And then they can say it out loud, and if someone's leading people the wrong way, I could overrule it. Say, "I think what you did was good; you don't have to do that with the color." And say *why*.

BEN: **Is there a classroom moment you can think of, either as a student or as a teacher, that sticks out to you as something you always go back to?**

DOUG: I had Dan Friedman as a teacher. And in some ways, Dan was somewhat reticent. He knew what he believed in, but he had difficulty sometimes saying it. And he was extremely respectful of our work. At that time, we were doing a lot of painting with brushes and paint. So he would always say, "Can I work on your work?" For some people, it bugged them. But for me, I thought this was good.

He would sit there and start working on my project, and he would be mixing colors, and I would ask him, "Well, why are you adding that color?" which made him nervous, I think. He just wanted to sit there and do it.

Thinking back I thought, this is good— I have surrendered my project to him. He's actually painting on my project, which is an unbelievable thing. And so I have always felt that I could actually take over. And sometimes I do. I say, "Give me the mouse. Can I do something to your project?" And I would. But if somebody says "no" to me, then I say, "OK, here's what I want you to do. I want you to do this, this, and this." And then I'll come back and look at it. But I liked that Dan did that.

Sometimes I, well, I rip up people's work. I think that's good too. Because I really feel that's a fast way to work with your hands, to see what something would look like.

BEN: **Not ripping it up to throw it out?**

DOUG: No, ripping it up to improve it. That's a way of working, a collage process in graphic design we can use more than anything. I had teachers who would break my models sometimes. And as I remember, the teacher always said, "Can I break this edge off?" Which I also do in Exhibit

Design. I do the same thing now, because we're working in three dimensions.

Dan was good. He was an interesting bird for me, because he wasn't as verbal as some of the other teachers. But he was intuitive, and he said a couple things to me that will always stick with me.

In our grad group, he mandated that we would cover all our desks in brown paper, and that came from his Basel experience, or at Ulm where he was before, where everything was just so. People wore lab coats. So he wanted that. He didn't want people putting too much stuff on their desks. It was a distraction. So we had to put stuff away, to set the stage where you can really focus.

Then one day he came over to me. We had a project where we had to make a grid and do an operation on the grid, and I thought it had to be logical. I was always being extremely logical. And he said, "OK, I see Step 1, Step 2, makes sense." Then he said to me, "I want you to go from Step 2 to Step 44." Or 43. I forget the number. And that completely tore down all of my logical thinking. But I began to think differently. And that was a huge day for me, where I realized that I didn't have to make everything regimentally logical. I could take great leaps. Be more expressive and intuitive.

The next thing he said was, "I know how you work. And I'm going to make a painter out of you." He was trying to make me be more expressive. Well, later that day, there was a woman who truly was a painter, before she came to Yale. And he was over there, and he said to her the magic words. He said, "I'm going to make an architect out of you." And I thought, "A-ha!" So it started making sense to me what the possibilities are here. He knew how to get us both working a different way.

BEN: **What compels you to teach?**

DOUG: I think most teachers are doing this because they want to help people get better at what they do. That's always been the drive for me. And that means teaching the things students need to learn that will allow them to continue to learn their entire lives, to become working professionals who are confident, and can also change and grow. I believe that we're not just training graphic designers, we're training human beings.

I think what compels me to teach, most of all, is to learn. I believe that the teacher always learns more than the students do. There are a whole bunch of points of view in the classroom, many different ways of doing things that the teacher probably wouldn't even dream of. You learn something every time you step into that room.

DOUGLASS SCOTT *has taught graphic design, exhibition design, typography, and graphic design history at the Rhode Island School of Design (since 1980), at the Yale University School of Art (since 1984), and at Northeastern University (since 2010). He was, until January 2010, creative director at the WGBH Educational Foundation in Boston—a producer and broadcaster of public television and radio programs—where he had worked since 1974.*

BENJAMIN SHAYKIN *is a Providence-based designer and educator who specializes in book design and other printed matter. In 2011, he received his MFA from the Rhode Island School of Design, where he now teaches typography, graphic design, and the future of the book. Previously, he was a designer and art director at* Chronicle Books and Mother Jones *magazine, and he was the founding creative director of the independent magazine* Bitch: Feminist Response to Pop Culture.

"It's okay to *break up* with your design. Remember when Ben and J-Lo broke up? See? You can find love again."

—KERMIT BAILEY
North Carolina State University
College of Design

"Are you a starter or a finisher? Many designers begin their careers being really strong at one and not the other. If you are great at both, rejoice! If not, know your weakness and exercise it like a muscle."

—DENNIS CROWE
California College of the Arts

"'Imagine filling in the space with ball bearings.'

When reviewing logotypes, I sometimes ask the students to turn the work upside down. This causes them not to read their type, but to see it purely as figure and ground. Now they should look at the optical volumes between each of the letterforms.

I ask them to imagine how many ball bearings can fit between each of the letterforms. In order to achieve a consistent optical spacing in the logotype, or text, there should optically be an equal amount of ball bearings between each of the letterforms.

This of course could work with envisioning water between the spaces as well.

This helps students to see the typography—to see the figure and ground relationships of letterforms when combined together, and to see what important kerning and spacing adjustments need to be made to achieve beautifully spaced logotypes."

—DAN HOY
Art Center College of Design

"Respect the reader. Type is meant to be read, first and foremost."

—PETER COCKING
Emily Carr University of Art + Design
Vancouver, BC

"Be generous with your appreciation, conversation, and collaboration. (Support the creative cause, critique and discuss freely, and collaborate often). This is about the importance of connecting with other creatives while helping foster a positive global art and design community. This is one of my personal mantras as well as a huge theme in my courses."

—LINDSAY NOHL
Minneapolis College of Art and Design

"Subtle changes make significant differences. This particularly applies to typography and the end stages of a design process. Fine tuning typography and design is about making subtle changes. It is with these final edits that a design can go from being good to great."

—CAROL SOGARD
University of Utah

Unipodial :: *by N. Silas Munro*

About half a year ago, an upper-level administrator of a prominent American art and design school said to me, "Let me ask you a nasty question." OK. It would have been impossible to predict being in this particular conversation.

I didn't reply right away. Instead, I took as smooth and deep a breath as I could muster. The administrator continued, "Do you really believe that your students get the same quality of education that our students or others in full-residency programs get?" I was surprised to be asked to defend what this administrator had requested to meet about in the first place—low-residency graduate education for designers. What surprised me more was what came out of my mouth. Beaming, with no hesitation, I said, "Yes!"

Some context: A year and a half prior, I was asked to join the founding faculty of a new low-residency MFA program in graphic design at Vermont College of Fine Arts (VCFA). Three weeks prior to meeting the aforementioned administrator, I was promoted to faculty chair of VCFA's design program. With our program in the middle of its second semester, I now found myself in hostile territory, asked to both explain and defend low-residency education everywhere.

I proceeded to try to make my face as soft and open as possible. It's the same face I attempt to make when a concerned graduate student in VCFA's program relays to me in a monthly check-in: "And then my partner said, 'Is that really graphic design, honey?' " I quickly and confidently explained the importance of student-centered independent study, the intimacy of the student to faculty ratios (5 to 1!), the unique administrators, and the innovative senior staff. It felt good to have this clarity about a program (and discipline) very much in flux.

We may be a young program—a young college, and I a young chair—and I might have surprised myself by what came out of my mouth. Once I sat down with this administrator and his team, however, I had no doubt what they were trying to do. They were trying to duplicate our model at VCFA. The problem is, how can anyone copy something that is still in formation? Simply put, you can't. Even as I write this, our program is still evolving and will continue to evolve. Even after our first graduation, in October, that evolution won't stop. In fact, once we stop evolving, we might as well close our doors.

Since this conversation with the administrator, I have been asked by a lot of people how a low-residency graduate program works, particularly in graphic design. I have a few oddball words that I use to try to capture the experience, but one of my favorite words was recently suggested to me by my colleague Natalia Ilyin during the end of our last residency. That word is *unipodial*.

A residency is a seven- to ten-day intensive that kicks-offs our six-month-long semesters. One of the things that makes a VCFA graphic design residency special is that there is one podium from which we all lecture: faculty, administrators, and, most important, students. We are a unipodial graphic design program. All week long, we balance on this one foot of communication, support, and trust.

When students and faculty return home for the six-month semesters, that unipodial energy continues. My colleague Geoff Halber described the VCFA semester like this: "Students work on their own, but with the close support of one faculty mentor at a time for each of their semesters at VCFA. As long as students are self-motivated, there are a number of benefits to this: they don't have to give up their entire lives to go to grad school (like most grad schools require); they aren't beholden to a particular kind of style, or pedagogy, or methodology (like most grad schools tend to formulate); and the students are free to guide their own course of study (unlike in most grad schools). Of course, students are supported by a wide-ranging faculty that have their own practices, and, equally so, the student body is unusually supportive of one another (less competitive/more encouraging), especially through a very active community of online networks."

The student work that I've seen so far has been broad. That is, everyone comes in with different strengths, interests, and capabilities. In our unipodial way, we tend to encourage students to find their own paths, and along those paths, we encourage them to do things they're not that comfortable doing or tend to avoid. It may not be a traditional approach to design education, but it's an approach that brings about compelling exploration and, sometimes, the most satisfying work.

N. SILAS MUNRO is faculty chair of the MFA program in graphic design at Vermont College of Fine Arts. His mission is in service of beautiful, smart design with empathy for humanity.

Before his current practice, Munro was design director at Housing Works in New York, designer-in-residence at North Carolina State, and design fellow at the Walker Art Center in Minneapolis. He holds an MFA and a BFA in graphic design from CalArts and the Rhode Island School of Design, respectively.

Based in Miami, Munro's Poly-Mode creates design for varied audiences across media that has won awards from ADC, AIGA, Print, and SAPPI Ideas that Matter. Silas's writing about design has been published by GOOD, NC State, and the Walker *Gradient*.

"THE BEST DESIGN IS INVISIBLE."

—JAYME ODGERS
California Institute of the Arts

"This is my twentieth year teaching courses in graphic design at California College of the Arts in San Francisco. I give my students no end of advice, I'm sure, but the one question I continually ask them that seems worth sharing is: 'Where does your eye go?' If you know where the eye goes when you look at work, and why, then you understand true hierarchy— regardless of the design intention. If you remain unaware of hierarchy, of what the eye sees and in what order, your work will remain indistinct and forgettable."

—MARK FOX
California College of the Arts

"Originality is good; effectiveness and appropriateness might be better.

The point being that we often dismiss work as derivative or 'of a style' before considering what it might accomplish in real terms of need and use."

—RODERICK GRANT
OCAD University, Toronto, ON

"Determination is often more important than talent."

—LOU DANZIGER
Art Center College of Design

"Being a designer is like having a new pair of eyes that are able to look at things that everybody sees from a different angle. Learning how to do that is the little magical outcome of long, long training."

—MARTA BERNSTEIN
Politecnico di Milano, Italy

Pirco Wolfframm interviewed by Leigh Mignogna and Liz Selbert

Recorded 12/22/12

LEIGH: One reason we like you as a professor is that you seem to have strong opinions and, more than other professors, you're not afraid to express them. As students in the midst of forming our own opinions and values as designers, this is really refreshing. Are you consciously opinionated in the classroom, or is it just part of your personality that comes through?

PIRCO: It is probably part of my personality, given my upbringing in a family with very strong opinions. As an undergraduate designer, I was extremely judgmental. I just would not want to associate with people if I thought of them as "bad" designers/artists/filmmakers. I learned to listen to my peers and to embrace other people's approaches in grad school as we learned to argue about the substance, the concept, and the content of a project in intense class discussions. There was no "thumbs up" or "thumbs down" verdict from faculty, which I was used to. Instead, we learned a nuanced way to argue, question, and constructively critique each other. When I started teaching, I realized how much I had learned in grad school by being able to argue distinctly and in a supportive but not directive manner. As a student, it is actually important to be exposed to different opinions, just the way you are exposed to different project solutions for the same project. These differences help negotiating towards your own way of thinking and making. If your learning is run by a uniform approach or an opinion-avoidance approach, you may have a hard time finding yourself in your design practice. You may not even allow yourself to have an opinion, and the reality is that everybody has one—it is just more or less pronounced.

LIZ: **Are there particular professors you learned that from along the way, or did you learn mostly from other students?**

PIRCO: During my undergraduate studies, I chose to stick with the professor who was most hands off, but with high expectations. During my graduate studies at CalArts, we were taught to "walk the walk and talk the talk." While it was great to learn the vocabulary to argue design in a certain way, it was difficult to evolve from there. We were in the midst of the postmodern discourse, and our faculty had been part of changing the discourse into that particular direction.

LIZ: **Did you oppose that mindset you were being taught?**

PIRCO: I embraced it and I also resisted it. On one hand, it was really exciting to learn how people can look at and think about design. Scrutinizing design along rhetorical means, semiotics, or looking at the audience, or relating graphic design to other cultural activities was eye opening. On the other hand, I felt that walking the walk and talking the talk was not yet an integral part of me, that I had not yet made it mine. It was still a pair of crutches.

LIZ: **What years were you at CalArts?**

PIRCO: I was at CalArts from '96 to '98. Their reputation had been established for a while, and I was curious to learn more about their ideas about design given their publications in *Emigre* magazine. I was attracted by the visual examples I saw but also by the writings of faculty.

LIZ: **You mentioned before that Jeff Keedy, Lorraine Wild, and Ed Fella were the main people there at the time.**

PIRCO: They were the three people who ran the seminar class which for us at Pratt equals thesis class.

LIZ: **Would you say that they defined the CalArts style at that time?**

PIRCO: They were the people who defined the program. The issue of style was an intensely discussed topic. From the outside CalArts appeared to be a school with a particular visual coherence described as 'style'. From the inside we all thought of ourselves as idiosyncratic individuals and would wildly experiment and search for our specific styles.

LIZ: **When you look back on that style now, how do you regard that work and what comes to mind? Also, related to that question: Do you see remnants of that style in other work now, or the work that you do, or in contemporary design? Or is that something that you feel has had its time and is now preserved in the past?**

PIRCO: The work as part of that style is preserved in the past, though the ideology as part of that style is still part of the general discourse. Historically, I still love a lot of the work. Personally, I embrace aspects such as complexity, multiplicity, and ambiguity in form and concept. Also, playing with typography gives me great pleasure. I still use typefaces as an expressive form and have a hard time using just one typeface. I tend to use at

least two, if not three [laughs]. I'm not particularly intrigued with the austerity and default aesthetic that I see a lot. It reminds me of an even farther away past.

LIZ: **As in Modernism?**

PIRCO: Not Modernism, but rather Fluxus or Conceptual Art. It's funny to me, I see quite a lot of design where I think, "This looks so old to me."

LEIGH: **What are your opinions about so-called "default design"?**

PIRCO: I still have a hard time wrapping my head around "default design." The approach is quite contrary to my Postmodern upbringing. Liz, you had a fantastic explanation (in one of your seminar writings), and to me, it's an interesting response to our current environment. Coming to design with an urge to communicate specifically, the term and often the visual quality bothers me, though. I love all aspects of form giving and I do want to communicate through specific form. The Modernist and the Postmodernist in me wants to see as many elements of design as possible being consciously used. Hence, default setups appear listless to me even though I know it's a form of critique.

LEIGH: Are there other things you see coming out of MFA programs that surprise or anger or confuse you?

PIRCO: The work seems very heady. You read a lot, and you have to digest all these theories and discussions. To a certain degree, this influx inhibits you from form-making as usual, because you become so conscious of it and you question every step you take with your projects. It's hard to integrate these constant impressions into your deliberate form giving and not let it limit you. In terms of outcome in MFA programs, I find form giving to be a weakness; it seems to be least discussed, partially due to an emphasis on very concept-heavy development and little time for execution and formal experimentation.

LEIGH: In one of the seminar classes, you asked us to define what a graphic designer is today. Did any of the results surprise you?

PIRCO: There were no particular surprises, but a good reflection of what graphic design currently defines itself as. I could sense that lot of people still come from Modernist-influenced upbringing in their design education and that default design or other system-based approaches are on people's minds as are collaborative processes and questions of social responsibility. With that, a fairly clean and lean and very structured design aesthetic seems to dominate. I also noticed students being occupied with the idea of the designer as an artist. It's not unusual, but it is interesting that it's so narrowed down to art. Where is designer as filmmaker? Where is designer as performer or politician? Those are equally valid options.

LIZ: It seems like that's a conversation within MFA programs and not necessarily undergrad or after.

PIRCO: Yes, I think it's important for graduate students to constantly question. "What am I doing here, and who am I doing it for?" Given that situations change, the environment changes, and technology changes, we are a very adaptive, chameleon-like profession. We need to look at the ecosystem around us, because we fulfill a role within it. But the way we fulfill it has to change all the time. Grad school is a great place to help define/redefine our practice.

LEIGH: In grad school right now, we have the luxury of figuring out what we like in design and what we're interested in—and that's really nice, but here's this fear that once we get outside of school, everything else will be a

disappointment. That if you're lucky enough to find your voice in design, you won't necessarily be able to follow it, because you'll have to (like you say) be a chameleon and fulfill all these roles. Is that something you had to adjust to after grad school, or do you feel that's an unnecessary fear to have?

PIRCO: In grad school, you live an intensely focused life with a community of similar concerns. It helps finding who you are as a person and as a designer. With the specific worldview and ideals you developed, it is at times hard to find the fitting employer. Some people are able to transition into a satisfying practice from the beginning of their work lives. It took me a while to find my preferred practice. I really wanted to live in New York, but it is a tricky place to make a living and to establish your practice as you want it. I was thrilled about my first job, at a web development company, which was a fairly new part of design practice, and excited to be in the midst of this new branch of design. At the same time, it was a business environment with roles to be performed, and its "walking the walk and talking the talk" to be learned. So the discussion about design and what it means and how it relates to other cultural activities, the whole beloved discourse, was unwanted and not billable. What counted was swift delivery of multiple concepts to choose from. The argumentation about our designs remained on the basis of what "looked good" or was "too far out." Even within the design department, the interest in the design field was limited. Hence, finding your niche, where you have projects that you love, causes that you care for, and where you have the exchange you look for is a project in itself. You need to find people with similar interests, go to events, etc., which can be quite demanding if you have enough work and a social life with not just designers.

LEIGH: **Do you have any strategies for yourself now to stay connected to the design you like?**

PIRCO: I'm someone who for a long time took design jobs often just to pay my bills. I'm not leading a glamorous life, just a basic one. For a while I did what Ed (Fella) calls "hacking." I did a lot of it and still do it to supplement my other activities in the field. It is the "bread and butter" portion of my existence. I found my interest in design in different types of projects, some personal and some for causes that I cared for, sometimes only parts of projects. I had projects where I really enjoyed working with a client, or where I had a lot of leeway, or once in a while you will have a project that you really love and care for. You may want to propose projects instead of waiting for them to come to you. You have to find something within any project that satisfies you. In the "bread and butter" world I prefer the process of research and ideation. In Germany, we say, "You can't always pick the raisins from the cake." I'm not sure if there is an equivalent in English. You need to fully cherish the parts that give you pleasure in your design practice. Teaching is a complementary activity to designing. The discussions in the graduate program are quite invigorating, and they challenge me. It took me a while to get back into the rigorous walk and talk after interacting with undergraduate students for a long time. I had to brush up my "vocabulary." Last summer, in preparing a reader for seminar class, I spent an entire month just reading and catching up with essays past and present. I loved curating the readings and developing related assignments. But it is interesting to notice how you can lose touch; having a circle of people to talk to about design, keeping up with the cultural production around us and staying engaged, is important.

LEIGH: I appreciated that you brought style up in one of my final critiques. You were the only professor who used that word, and it's nice to have someone say that we can talk about developing a style. I think its something that people avoid, because in some sense you should approach every design problem with fresh eyes.

LIZ: Style is a tricky word, because it depends how you define it. You can easily mean just this surface-level thing, or it can be how you approach problems. And that doesn't mean it always has to look the same. Your way of thinking can be a style.

PIRCO: Exactly. Massimo Vignelli uses less than five typefaces in his entire practice. You can call that a style. I also use less than five typefaces, but I use them all together in one project. And all of them are different in each project for specific reasons. You can call that style, too, even though it won't be as visually recognizable as Mr. Vignelli's approach. I find style a highly interesting topic, particularly in light of the surge of default systems design approaches and collaborative experiments we see right now. There is still style there, but it is not driven by the individual designer controlling every detail. Letting go of control and opening the project up to algorithms or design partners is style in itself as a way of thinking but also formally.

LIZ: You had Ed Fella in for a class, via Skype, and we all really enjoyed hearing him talk. He's such a great personality and has a really healthy perspective on design. It seems like he had quite an influence on you as a graduate student. Was there something particular about him as a teacher that you liked and try to emulate?

PIRCO: There were three core teachers and a mentor. I connected most to Ed, because he was an easygoing, constant presence in his studio, which was situated inside our space. I appreciated his encouraging comments as we also got a lot of (very helpful) nagging questions when presenting our work. I learned from that. When I critique work, I tend to first look for the questions that arise. He pointed out the aspects that were working and that were beautiful. So I remind myself a lot to address the aspects that work well, that surprise and that delight.

Ed and the others were great at providing contextual references, to situate our project in the microcosm and macrocosm of design. And he is not caught up in his own celebrity-reputation preservation. It was really useful to understand how unconcerned he is about the way other people see him, because I was a bit starstruck when I first met him and my other professors. Mainly, he was an acknowledging, trusting

peer, not a "higher authority," and I try to interact with my students similarly. He was just there and approachable. I learn from students just as much. They have interesting opinions to develop and to prove, and my involvement is that I have a different set of eyes, a different attention to detail, and a different experience to offer, so they can evolve their projects.

LEIGH: Have there been any students of yours who you feel you especially learned from or who have affected the way you teach?

PIRCO: There are lots of students that I really enjoyed working with. I cherish students who engage and really care for what they are studying. It is great to see people struggle and fight through their projects or writings and then evolve from there. I can't say I've learned from a particular student, but rather types of situations. It is invigorating when classes develop a nurturing and challenging dynamic. I've had classes that were just unbelievable. It was wonderful to see students running their class almost on their own, because a few of them were just so eager to get certain things discussed and their enthusiasm was contagious to the others. On occasion, I have adjusted my courses— for example, due to inflexibility. I try to steer students on a more scenic route when exploring a project. The whole idea of focusing on process in my undergraduate senior-project class stems from seeing students execute their first idea based on preconceptions instead of learning about the subject matter, the audience, etc., and then testing multiple options. Maybe they have learned to go for the quick answer from other classes. But I say, "No, think about it. Start asking questions first."

LEIGH: I think that's really important. As a student, the assignments where I've learned the most are the ones where I've tried ten different ways. You learn from what doesn't work rather than accepting your first answer as being the best.

PIRCO: Fear of failure is a huge issue. Partly because education costs so much, and students don't want to get bad grades as that's tied to financial support. But failing is so important in relation to learning. I don't know if it's generational or if it is indeed a matter of economics, but people don't allow failure to happen as much anymore.

LIZ: What are the three most important things you want students to come away with in your classes?

PIRCO: For each class, there are different learning goals, and assignments are different steps towards those specific goals. In undergrad, I want people to think critically and flexibly, besides just gaining skills. At large, I think it is important for students to come away with the idea that, if they understand how to create meaningful messages in a specific context, they have an immensely broad platform of opportunities for their future work, whether it is graphic design or not. Understanding how to facilitate communication visually as well as verbally, gives you a huge advantage over people who are geeks in their field. I also long for beauty and hope students manage to use the urge for beauty in congruence with meaning. To understand that their graphic design education is a starting point to evolve as a person as well as a professional, not an end point, is really important.

LEIGH MIGNOGNA *and* **LIZ SEIBERT** *are recent graduates of Pratt's MFA communications design program. Both are freelance designers living and working in New York.*

PIRCO WOLFFRAMM *is a graphic designer and design educator. She moved from Germany to the U.S. with a fellowship to obtain her MFA degree at CalArts. Besides her design practice, she teaches in the Pratt Graduate Communications Design program, New York, and occasionally at MICA, Baltimore. Her designs and writings on design have been exhibited and published in Europe and the U.S. She recently co-authored and designed the book* Eva Zeisel: Life, Design, and Beauty.

"If you're going into design for the money, you won't make any money at it."

—**STEVEN SKAGGS**
Hite Art Institute,
University of Louisville

"I want you to put your hand over your heart and promise that, as long as you live, you will never, never, indent a first paragraph again."

—DEBBIE ADAMS

OCAD University, Toronto, ON

"WHEN IN DOUBT, EDIT IT OUT."

—CAROL SOGARD
University of Utah

"Ask for what you want, sieze opportunities when they come your way, and be daring with all of your endeavors."

—LINDSAY NOHL
Minneapolis College of Art and Design

"Know when to stop. If the content is strong, sometimes the best solution is to call it done and send out an invoice."

—PETER COCKING
Emily Carr University of Art + Design
Vancouver, BC

"EXPLORE, PLAY, REFLECT—AND GET YOUR HANDS INTO IT!"

—JESSICA BARNESS
School of Visual Communication Design
Kent State University

P. Scott Makela :: *by Brett MacFadden*

I thank Scott Makela, who by being here my first year
taught me much, and by not being here my second, taught
me everything else. Scott, you are in us all.

• • • • •

That quote is from the acknowledgments in my graduate thesis. Recently, I met with a designer who was thinking of attending the Cranbrook Acadaemy of Art, from where I graduated in 2000. He wanted my thoughts on the experience more than ten years out of the garden. So I did a little homework and reread my thesis. I have to say I was delighted. It was a little precocious, sure, and the design work was frequently awful. But it was a good, snappy manuscript, truly beautiful at points. I'm not embarrassed to say I tear up every time I read it. I had that rare and wonderful experience of being inspired by one's own work, as if a ghost from the past came to help me believe in the future.

Because of rereading my thesis, I thought about that time when I was right at the doorstep of something new. About the power of change, the promise of the future, and the ghosts of the past. Many of you are in that time now. So today I'd like to talk about one of my ghosts—my teacher P. Scott Makela.

All teachers haunt students. It's one of the great joys of teaching, as well as of learning. As a teacher, knowing that when a student is off in the world your spirit will suddenly whisper in her ear, "Be sure and haaaaaang your punctuation."

But Scott Makela is more of a ghost than most teachers, because he died in 1999, at the age of thirty-nine.

I knew Scott for less than a year, and he and I were never close. In his personal-slash-professional life he tended to favor students who could keep up with him. Usually those who were already quite experienced, who could design on his terms—as big, as bold, as strong, bright, loud, powerful, as possible. I went to grad school, having studied journalism as an undergrad and having worked in marketing. I hoped school would give me the refined chops of a professional. Scott was way beyond the quest for refinement. He wanted horsepower. Here in metropolitan Detroit, Scott was a muscle car in the home of muscle cars.

And I was a bit of an import.

While discussing potential subjects for this talk, my business partner, Scott Thorpe, pointed out that few design students today would be familiar with Makela. Later, at our studio, I asked a young designer if he knew who P. Scott Makela was. He responded, "Who?"

• • • • •

As a design practitioner, I don't have many ghosts of teachers past. Because I studied journalism as an undergrad and never practiced it, those teachers don't visit me much. And because I went to Cranbrook, where there is no coursework and where each department typically has only one instructor, there are relatively few voices to follow me around. At the time, the graphic design department was unusual in that it had two instructors, called artists-in-residence, and those instructors were married to each other. Laurie and Scott Makela were incredibly close and a study in the power of contrast. Laurie's early work was delicate and typographically noodled. One of my prized possessions is a series of books she did for the Getty Center in the late '80s and early '90s.

The books are classically elegant and, yet, allow for oddity and drama. Scott, on the other hand, was the very definition of ADD. You could almost say he was attention-enabled. His work never struggled against the limitations of focus, but rather took full advantage of a scanning mind. It was produced quickly and often consumed in the same way. As teachers, they naturally took on good-cop, bad-cop roles. With Scott, he would come in, see what you were doing, get really excited, and generally tell you to keep going, amp it up! Scott was the voice of passion. Of fun, and go for it. But with that came the sense sometimes of getting off too easily.

Laurie was the taskmaster. I'd get nervous when she came to my desk, knowing that she was not as likely as Scott to get swept up in her own enthusiasm. Although every bit as passionate as Scott in her own work, in the studio she was the voice of seriousness and duty. Of work harder, and of try again.

I think we all felt lucky to have this two-sided arrangement in our department. There was a clear sense of family—of surrogate parents—and it meant that a greater variety of artistic voices might fight representation, that there was no true instructional voice of God. It's probably no surprise then, that as a teacher and practitioner, I've gravitated toward working with a partner with whom our system is equal parts encouragement and debate.

Because Scott is dead, and because the experience was a decade ago, it's hard for me to accurately say what I thought of him when I was his student. Now I admire him immensely. Now he seems like a remarkable gift of a person. Full of power and life until, suddenly, he wasn't. But at the time, he was more of a rare presence. He was often away lecturing and had a busy practice, so we saw him infrequently—perhaps once a week, often less. He cared about us, to be sure, but like any teacher, he had a lot of ducklings. He fed those he could.

If I picture him in class critique, I see him making wisecracks. He has spiky blond hair, these futuristic-looking swoopy glasses. His body is sturdy and compact in an untucked dress shirt, jeans, and chunky skateboard sneakers. Totally at home with who he is.

In my head, he's sort of leaned back in the crit room, one foot up on the bench. Even then, even now, he seemed a little cooler than the rest of the room. As a teacher, surrounded by people half my age, as Scott often was, I now recognize you can only pull that off if it's effortless and true. Scott and Laurie were minor celebrities in our midst. And, as I suspect is often the case with access to genuine celebrities, we found them to be surprisingly normal, and yet not at all.

It's hard to describe Scott without resorting to some analogy of his force. I could easily see him reincarnated as a pit bull. Not a fighting dog—Scott was aggressive, not violent—more the kind that is loving and sweet and occasionally humps your sofa. Then consumes it. Like a pit, Scott was meaty and strong and always straining at the leash. Lorraine Wild called him "just a barrel of energy." Paul Schneider, a student who also worked for Scott's studio, said, "Scott was a power-chord designer. He'd get the biggest amp and pick you could find and go 'blam!' "

Scott's work—their work—fundamentally, is why I wanted to study with Scott and Laurie. The work had an intensity and power and mysticism that was profoundly seductive. It was often considered ugly and raw. And it often *was* ugly and raw. Type ran over type, headlines were centered in the page. Bold on top of bold. Italic and underlined. Red and yellow and blue and metallic gold. He may have been among the last generation of graphic designers who truly felt what they were doing was new. When computers and the Internet were still a bit *Mad Max*, and Scott could be called a "cyberpunk" in *Eye* magazine and not have it sound totally phony.

Scott was well-known for the speed with which he designed. This was sometimes a response to deadlines, but also to his own thrum and mindset. His work encapsulated the rate at which it was produced, the page or screen packed with vibrancy. In a 1992 *Emigre* article, he said, "I am trying to grab a chunk of experience and have it bleed off all edges."

• • • • •

Imagine the sound that happens when an unmuffled motorcycle goes down the street, and all the car alarms yelp out in the backwash. Scott's work met some of the same response in design circles. It was vigorously hated at times—representative of an ivory-tower approach to chaos that would filter down until every cereal box and every hometown newspaper was an overwhelming mishmash of fonts, colors, and sloshy jpegs.

In the early '90s, after several years running a studio in Los Angeles, Scott and Laurie went to study at Cranbrook. Describing that time, in *Eye*, Scott said, "I was interested in work that had a certain sensuality in it, that might have room for independence and a kind of tribalism. At Cranbrook we were all little one-person tribes, and I was the first wire-head."

As a wire-head, a cyberpunk, Scott was an early adopter of everything, and as his work quickly moved into motion and sound, he always needed a computer more powerful than the last. There's that analogy about only using 10 percent of our brain, and I suspect most of us increasingly use only a small part of the true processing power that our computers are blessed with. But with Scott, particularly at that time, his work pushed the very limits of commercial machines. Looking at some of the early work with today's eyes, it doesn't seem like such a big deal to produce. We can deconstruct it and think, oh, blur filter. But blur filter was high technology at the time, pre-digital camera, made for gently softening images, not typography. And it was a render that was slow and likely to crash a system. Photoshop 1.0 came out in 1990, about the time Scott would have been designing the 1991 and 1993 course catalogs for his alma matter, the Minneapolis College of Art and Design. The later catalog probably would have been produced on something like the top-of-the-line Mac Quadra 900m, a computer that cost $8,500 without a monitor (roughly $13,000 today). It was the first Mac to be built as a tower, it had a 25-MHz processor, and it shipped with 4 MB of RAM. Yet somehow, he was blurring images, rendering 3D typography, and creating custom fonts. Part of the draw of Scott's design is the miracle that it could be done at all.

Scott's work on the 1995 Michael Jackson video for "Scream" is one of my favorite examples of his typography-meets-technology approach. At $7 million, it was, until recently, the most expensive video ever made, and thankfully, some of that beautiful budget went toward innovative graphic design. The opening title has a puffed up rendering of Scott's font "Dead History" as a glossy silver gate that splits open to let us in. Throughout the video, his typography plays a prominent role, flying through the galaxy with Michael and Janet on their spaceship.

Seductive was a favorite term. A lot of designers question their medium's ability to provoke emotion. But with Scott, it was the essential quality. The "payload," in his lingo. Often the job of design—particularly when teamed with advertising—is to seduce. To make you love and want something you may not have loved and wanted thirty seconds ago. For Scott, it was more personal, sometimes more raunchy. He was nothing if not sexual, and the idea of seduction was native to his process. Scott took open delight in boobs and butts and the sacred act, and sex was often mined for material, such as on the cover of their book *Where Is Here* [*Whereishere*?], featuring a blurred and brightly colored porn still. And if one side was sex (the profane), the other was spirit (the sacred). As a teenager in Minnesota, he embraced Christianity, even at one point joining a heavy-metal Pentecostal band. He's quoted in *Eye* as saying, "I am a deeply religious person about whatever I feel at that moment . . . it's just that it changes quickly."

While the sacred and profane are traditionally positioned as opposite poles, I think Scott saw them as complimentary routes on the road to gratification—representative of fulfillment's lifelong chase and a peeling away of our clothed, civic, and civil life toward something richer and harder to know.

When I interviewed for admission to Cranbrook, the process required that I meet with each current student in the studio and then, at a designated time, meet with Laurie and Scott in their separate workspace. We talked about meditation and Buddhism, which they had come to practice, and about the relationship of spirituality to work. Laurie and Scott designed around mantras—"Live to Death," "Select Your Network," "Flesh and Fluid"—and students naturally found their own: reinforcements of a conceptual position, a form of poetry to charge the design. The title of Laurie and Scott's book, *Where is Here*, for example, comes from a visit to Laurie's brother, a Zen monk in Korea. There, she learned about wordless teaching and the demonstrative argument, tools used to sharpen the mind. In her introduction to the book, she recalls: "What is this?" (the Zen master asks his student), holding up one finger. With the speed and precision of dueling swords, the student answers, "This." "Where is here?" he asks, looking the student in the eye. The student answers, "Here."

It's common to hear Cranbrook compared to a monastery, or just as often, a cult. I had spent close to ten years in the working world, wearing slacks, writing proposals, running to FedEx. I was ready for change, and a monastery sounded about right, a cult not that bad either. Scott and Laurie offered the study of something bigger than vocational training. It was a belief in the power of belief and that graphic design has all the tools needed to make that journey.

• • • • •

In Michigan, the long, gray winters seem to turn a page in April, and the landscape snaps from bleak to lush. With a semester that ends in early May, this leaves just a couple weeks of luxury, perversely timed with the heaviest workload of the year. It was during this sweet and floral season that I entered the studio on May 5 to find my classmates in shock. Standing at a wide-open door that framed a fresh green lawn, I learned that Scott was in a coma. A rare infection of the epiglottis—the flap in your throat that routs air to the lungs—had blocked his breath. Two days later, with recovery impossible, life support was cut. Two days after that, Laurie's brother, the monk, traveled from Seoul to lead a memorial held on that same bright new grass. Graduation ceremonies were held three days after that, on May 12.

For Scott, like many of us here, his work and his life were intertwined. And so, faced with an inconceivable loss, we retreated into graphic design. We made T-shirts.

Really.

The shirts said, "There's 3D Type in the Sky" and were designed by our fellow student Warren Corbitt, a friend and collaborator of Scott's, and set in Detroit—an aggressive typeface that had become Scott and Laurie's go-to in recent times. I wore mine for years, until it was faded and stained, the ink cracked and illegible. And then one day I stopped. Now it sits at the bottom of my drawer, and perhaps it always will.

• • • • •

In January 2011, the Museum of Modern Art in New York delighted type lovers by formally acquiring digital fonts into its permanent collection. Stated curator Paola Antonelli: "This first selection of twenty-three typefaces represents a new branch in our collection tree. They are all digital or designed with a foresight of the scope of the digital revolution, and they all significantly respond to the technological advancements occurring in the second half of the twentieth century. Each is a milestone in the history of typography."

Among these milestones were two typefaces born from Laurie and Scott. Matthew Carter's 1995 face, Walker, was commissioned by Laurie while she was design director of the Walker Art Center in Minneapolis, and it set the bold tone of work to come. The other face, Scott's 1990 Dead History, was originally formed while he was a student at Cranbrook by mashing up two "dead faces"—Centennial and V.A.G. Rounded—to give birth to one that MOMA calls "something entirely new and unexpected." It was released as a commercial face by Emigre in 1994, and it is still available through Emigre for purchase. That Dead History would become history itself is a pleasure we can all enjoy.

Scott taught us that design can be personal and powerful. Ballsy and loud with the throttle wide open. He taught us that nothing is timeless, and to take joy and nourishment from the vapor of your era. As makers, we operate in a fortunate sphere. We won't last, but in some form, our work likely will. And our ghosts will thrive for years to come.

BRETT MACFADDEN is a partner in the San Francisco–based design studio MacFadden & Thorpe.

"Curiosity is your best design skill. Nurture it. Protect it from judgment."

—AMBER HOWARD

North Carolina State University
College of Design

"When a student is pursuing their solution in a rather narrow way, I might say, 'Get some chocolate in your peanut butter!'"

—BOB AUFULDISH
California College of the Arts

"When indecisive, trust your instincts. You've honed them all your life."

—BRAD BARTLETT
Art Center College of Design

"Trust the design process—research, explore (concept development), select, compose, refine. Those various steps will help you develop successful solutions. Always allow time to step back and reflect at all stages of the project."

—LESLIE FRIESEN
Hite Art Institute,
University of Louisville

STOP. :: *by Leslie Becker*

FORMATIVE MOMENTS

1964. Hannes Beckmann was my 2D Studies professor. This was during the heyday of the East Village, psychedelic graphics and fashion, and experimental theater. He was a German émigré from the Bauhaus. (No, really, from the Bauhaus.) I took great care with my projects. Professor Beckmann even asked to copy my notes at the end of the semester because they were so detailed and thorough. He also was in the habit of locking the classroom door promptly at the beginning of every class (trains running according to schedule). I can say with relative certainty that I was one of his favorite students. One morning, I appeared in class wearing extremely discordant colors and patterns (the David Carson of fashion, the end of taste). He removed me into the hallway outside of the classroom and simply said in his thick German accent, "Miz Feiner (my name at the time), you know better than this."

1965. Ed Colker was my graphic design professor. I would often walk up the long flights of stairs to our classroom on the fifth floor of Cooper Union's landmark Foundation Building. This particular morning, I had dropped my 15-by-20-inch illustration board, denting the corner. Upon arrival in the classroom, I attempted to flatten the dented board before hanging it on the wall for review. My critique time arrived. Professor Colker looked at my project and asked me a few questions. Did I think the angle of the dent was right? And what about the depth of the dent? After a well-timed pause, he looked at me and asked, "Get it?"

Ongoing: time to imagine. Even while working on the simplest of projects, not only did I have to think and plan before making anything, I also had to go to the art-supply store and assemble all of my supplies. Often, while staring at the selection of papers, I had to imagine what my project would look like if I used this paper as opposed to that one. If I needed information, I had to make time to go to the library. Time was wrapped into the entire arc of the process of making. STOP.

1979 on. I begin teaching and realize that this is the real beginning of my education.

(late) 1980s. San Antonio, AIGA. Neville Brody urges designers to THINK, THINK THINK. . . . (Therefore, the plea is really not new.)

1990s on. Scavenging/Internet design—not designing the Internet, but designing from the Internet. With the DIY-ism, in a world of self-publishing, blogging, screen captures, has design become scavenging? STOP.

1996. University of California at Berkeley. One of my classmates was a young Polish woman who had done her undergraduate work in architecture. She presented one of our class projects using a foam head. Her choice of material infuriated our professor but delighted her. An enormously rigorous thinker, she strongly and articulately defended her choice. In Poland, she and her architecture classmates could make models only if they first made their own boards. She described the patience required in order to make the boards sufficiently sturdy. "Lots of vodka was consumed," she said, "as we waited for each layer of the paper to dry." STOP.

2000. Many of us, as faculty, are working with a distinct advantage. We have the good fortune of having lived through a time when there were burdens of financial costs and time consumption that resulted from carelessness during the design process. I realize that I arrive at the screen with entirely different educational and professional backgrounds from my students. I am still working to figure out what that means. I can't live their lives, and they can't live mine. I know what I know, but do I know what they know? If everyone is designing (i.e., DIY), what does it mean to go to school to study design? What should the knowledge look like?

SOME QUASI-RANDOM THOUGHTS AND OBSERVATIONS

The overvaluing of surface. I think we understand generally that surface has taken the prize in research and design. But why (or) does this matter? And what, if anything, should we do about it?

Is design now simply the ability to differentiate from among many situations and possibilities?

In an increasingly editor-free world, is design simply editing (not to imply that good editing is that simple)?

Iteration redefined. Digital environments imply iteration, simply because of the ease of interaction with the technology. But there may be two vastly different and time-dependent definitions of iteration:

> Iteration 1.0. It used to imply an evaluation of something, a revisiting, and then an alteration (hopefully improved) to the previous version.

> Iteration 2.0. Iterative has a new meaning that does not necessarily imply improvement, but rather simply another thing occurring chronologically. It is often not even a version of the prior thing, not even "new and improved."

What happens to design if the iterative process tends toward elimination of that critical piece that demands thoughtful review, reflection, and self-evaluation as part of the process?

Speed and lack of care. Talk on the phone anywhere. Photograph anytime. Share everything. Brain and hand disconnect. Touch-screen culture. Drag with abandon. Make before thinking. Where does value live in a virtual world?

I capture, therefore I design.

I curate, therefore I design. Has casual curatorial activity of someone else's "stuff" come to define design practice?

There is no longer cost or consequence resulting from carelessness. How do we (or should we) arrest the culture of marginalized care and specificity? What happens to design when the consequences of design are perceived as inherently trivial because of their temporality?

This is not about the "good old days." This is about the persistent value in doing something well. I suggest that one of our critical tasks is to teach focus while working in the digital environment, because that is where most of "design doing" (from research to making) is "geographically" situated. Perhaps while moving around the screen, gazing at all of our menus and the seemingly endless visual options that we cannot possibly hold in our head simultaneously, thinking out loud may be the most useful of contemporary pedagogical practices. It is a vote for consciousness, presence, dialogue with students, and opportunities for explanation.

A life with constraints is a life well lived. It implies focus, connection, and respect for others.

I am not asking that we flatten the world. Design is many things, and it is constantly changing. What is the new relationship between thinking and making? How are care and carefulness (not cautiousness) valued?

How do we consider? Reflect? Imagine? How do we STOP ?

LESLIE BECKER, PHD and AIGA/SF Fellow, is a professor of graphic design and visual atudies, former director of design, and former chair of graphic design at California College of the Arts. Her research area is design and ethics, and her design practice includes writing, print, and furniture.

"GLOSSY (INVARIABLY) SUCKS!"

—**CLIVE PIERCY**
Art Center College of Design

"On process:

—Make first.

—Find a way out of your head."

—EMILY McVARISH
California College of the Arts

"Read the text before you start, and make sure you understand it. Draw your design out from within the content, rather than imposing an arbitrary solution on top of the material. That's not design, that's cake decorating."

—PETER COCKING

Emily Carr University of Art + Design
Vancouver, BC

"Design proceeds from a point of not knowing where it will end up—and as designers, we must be okay with that."

—CHARLES NIX
Parsons The New School for Design

INDEX

"PRACTICE SAFE DESIGN: USE A CONCEPT."

—PETRULA VRONTIKIS
Art Center College of Design